The Complete Guide T

# Successful Eating

*Making Eating Simple to Achieve Your Goals*

## Sean Lerwill

#BeMoreCommando

# Contents

# Introduction

Welcome to the "The Complete Guide to Successful Eating". By purchasing this book you have taken a big step towards changing your lifestyle. It's up to you by how much.

First, I want to explain that this book isn't a "diet". I'm not a fan of the conventional term diet or "a diet" and what it has come to mean. It is now synonymous with people cutting Calories or macros and basically stopping themselves having something or other for a period of time. It is also more often than not linked with people breaking or cheating on said "diet". People jump from one diet to the next, removing one food or another, all of which at some level is unhealthy to a point.

This book is different. It's not restrictive and as such isn't a diet, but before we get onto that, let's discuss the word diet. I want you to see this book and its message(s) more in the old terms of what the words "diet" meant, as in "meat free diet" or "dairy free diet" where the term diet simply describes how you choose to eat; not for a short period of time, but indefinitely. This book is designed to give you the tools to eat healthily but also to enjoy what you eat from now until, well, forever. In that sense it's a diet (way of eating) for life.

I'm a qualified teacher with a PGCE. I was trained to teach by the Royal Marines. I'm also a scientist (BSc Molecular Genetics) and the two combined have lead to a book that is based around imparting scientifically based nutritional ideas and concepts to you to enable you to live a healthy, fit and disease free lifestyle. I've also included sections on dos, don'ts, myths and rules to make things even clearer.

Towards the end of the book I have created some Example Menus. These are simply daily food intakes ideas based around Calorie amounts. The idea behind these menus is that they will supply you with all the Calories you need for a day based around your Calorie needs. Nutrition is not one size fits all. We all have different needs, whether these be down to our individual health and fitness goals or simply down to the size of our bodies.
One of the great things about these Example Menus is that to make them workable the foods are simple and basic, food is fuel after all. If you don't like the idea of eating simply, no problem. This book also contains all the info you need to create Calorie and macros goals for yourself based around your somatotype (body type) and utilise a Calorie tracker like MyFitnessPal to keep on track. If that's not for you though, then there are simply a set of health rules to follow for each meal that should see you improve both health and well being in a short space of time. These rules are a great way to begin a new way of eating, providing both honesty and integrity to the way you eat and all the pros that go along with eating a healthy diet.

I hope you can see from the outline of the book in this introduction that I take my Commando Values very seriously and thus try to ensure honesty and integrity throughout. This book is no different. I've tried to keep this as simple and therefore as short as possible, to give you the tools you need to eat for health, fitness and if you want, aesthetics.

We live in a very different world from 50 years ago, actually even 20 years ago! This can be good and bad. There are many, many great things about this day and age; smart phones, electric cars, medical science, on demand TV (the list goes on and on) but there are also two things that I believe are really negative about the current world we live in:

1.      Impatience.
1.      Pressure to look a certain way.

Impatience comes from a world where we can get what we want quickly and often easily. Information is literally at our fingertips as soon as it comes into our heads with the advent of smartphones. This can be great. If you wanted to know something you would previously have needed an encyclopaedia (what's that?!) or a dictionary for. These days, we just "Google" on our smartphone. This impatience has spread into other parts of our lives meaning in nearly everything we do there's increased expectation, impatience and wanting everything now!

No-one wants to wait for the effects of training or diet to take place. This is often because they've left it until 2 weeks before a summer holiday to "lose weight". The problem is that our bodies don't work that way. In my opinion, anything in this life worth having takes time, effort and hard work to get and therefore is something to be proud of. A lean figure/physique is something to be proud of and therefore takes time to achieve. Building muscle takes time, losing body fat (depending on how much you have to lose) takes time. Someone once said *"if you really want something, you'll make the time. If you don't, you won't"*. Do you really want to lose body fat, gain muscle or become healthier?

If you are impatient about your need to be lean/lose body fat, you won't give the plan you decide to create from this book enough time and thus you'll fail. Don't be impatient. The only person who can do this is you. You have to be strong, focussed, determined and see the bigger picture; the end goal. If you can do that, you'll be successful and have a figure/physique you'll be proud to show off at the beach along with a far healthier body under the bonnet. You will have made life changing habit changes that will see you being far healthier and thus living far longer while reducing the risk of lifestyle diseases like diabetes or heart disease. If that alone isn't enough to convince you, well, it should be.

This leads me onto the second point: pressure to look a certain way. If the world we live in didn't have that pressure, you wouldn't be reading this book. I want people to be able to be happy in the long term and to be able to get hold of the information you need to make the changes you want. At the outset this may be to become leaner/more toned or whatever you think you want. Beyond this, I have often found that if people reach their goal, or even part way, it adds self-confidence. This can help with reaching goals in other parts of their life: relationships, work etc. Reaching aesthetic goals (at least in the ways laid out in this book) can lead to a more confident, healthier and hopefully more disease free and happier life. If that wasn't the case, I wouldn't spend my time writing this book. For me, seeing people become happier and healthier makes writing books such as this worthwhile.

There are far too many people out there who are upset and depressed because they believe they can never look like this person or that person. Personally I believe you should never want to look like or be anyone else. However, I do think everyone deserves to be the very best person they can be; mentally, physically, emotionally etc. and these are often linked. Therefore, this book is designed to help you obtain a healthier, fitter, leaner, better performing and long lasting physique/figure, in a healthy way. If that's what you want.

## Aesthetics

If I think about the various people who have asked me for nutritional or training advice over the years, I would say 80-90% of people were looking for an aesthetic change. They wanted to look better. Even those wanting a nutritional plan for training for a marathon or a triathlon or to increase strength and conditioning for a sport, often started doing those events/sports with the aim for losing some "weight" and trying to look better. True, this isn't the case for all. In fact, many people I have worked with have been pursuing their sport/competition for years. Many have finally realised that improving their diet can improve their performance, but I also find that many take up that sport/activity to lose weight and therefore want to team it with a sensible nutritional plan.

What I have tried to do with each person I've worked with is help them understand the underlying reason as to why they want to be healthier or obtain a more aesthetic figure/physique. The two most common underlying reasons were to gain confidence and to be more attractive to potential partners. I can completely empathise with both. As a teen/young adult I was not very confident; I started on a fitness journey to improve my physique thinking (as I heard it did for Sylvester Stallone) that it would give me confidence despite the things I didn't like about myself. Largely, it did. I was also shy around women and the thought was that a muscular physique with a six pack like a Hollywood film star would help with that. To be honest, I'm not sure it has. The women I have been in relationships with have always maintained they don't really like muscular men and that wasn't a factor for them. Take from that what you will. What I would say is that if it gave me confidence and it was that confidence which they liked in me, in a roundabout way my fitness helped me. Who knows? Again, you have to understand what it is for you.

The bottom line is to really consider whether you will feel better about yourself if you change your body. If it will add confidence at work when giving presentations; in public when out and about or when trying to find a partner, or at interviews for promotions or a new job, then go for it. Use it as a reason not to give up and to do it 100%. If when you really look deep down, your appearance doesn't really worry you that much, consider why you are doing what you are doing. You don't need to follow a Calorie counting plan to be healthy; you can simply eat fresh, non-processed whole foods and have some thought about doing activity and exercise. That in itself would make you healthier. Is it health or aesthetics you really want? If it really is just health, then I would follow the "8 Simple Rules" and "20 Foods to Eat" below and leave the rest of the information in this book for if and when you decide to refocus.

Many nutritional advisors or fitness coaches shout that it should be health first and aesthetics will follow. I see where they are coming from; they are worried about the ever changing world in which aesthetics is more important than anything and thus anorexia, steroid use and other such unhealthy practices are common to simply produce the end goal of a great looking body. Sadly, with no concern for what is going on under the hood. I follow a different approach. The most recent nutritional course I studied was by Precision Nutrition and their philosophy is very much a tri-targeted approach:

1. Health
1. Performance
1. Aesthetics

The thought process being that by exercising sensibly (including resistance weighted exercise, LISS cardio and HIIT cardio) and combining this with a sensibly planned, nutritionally sound diet; anyone can improve health, performance and aesthetics all at once. That is exactly what we are going to do in this book; to give you the tools to create your very own sensibly planned, nutritionally sound diet.

## What to expect

I'm not going to "BS" you. This is not going to be a simple trick to get you lean and like a Men's Health/Victoria's secret model. It doesn't work like that. As I said above, anything worth having is hard to get. If it wasn't, everyone would have it and then it would cease to be special and then no-one would want it. So expect to work hard.

What I am going to do, is help you understand what it is your body needs and why there is no one size fits all. You can't do the same as your friend or mother or father or the person from the local gym who entered a bodybuilding contest and won a medal. It doesn't work like that. We all have different needs due to our size, weight, height, age and activity. Therefore we are going to take all that into account to help you work out what you need and to help you get it.
Furthermore, this isn't something I sell to you for 8 weeks or for 12 weeks only. This book can be used again and again. You can put the information about yourself into the formulas (if that side of things works for you) to come and work out what you need. If you train hard and eat right, you'll change those values (you'll lose body fat) so may have to work out new figures after a few months.

To keep this book short and sweet I am not going to go into great depth as to what macronutrients are (protein, carbs and fats), what micronutrients are, what vitamins, minerals and phytochemical are and various other components of science. I could. As mentioned, I have a post graduate certificate in education and a degree in Genetics. I am well versed in imparting knowledge and always aimed to do so when working with someone one to one, but to become healthier, more muscular or leaner, you don't NEED to know the science to that detail. In this book we want it to be simple and accessible, so we simply want you to have the info you NEED to make changes to your body.

# Chapter 1: Exercise

‿‿‿ᴏᴋ is about creating a nutritional plan that is as simple and easy to follow or as complex and specific as YOU need. In my opinion, too many people ignore nutrition thinking that spending all their time concentrating on exercise will allow them to eat whatever they want. Not so. To quote someone, somewhere: "You can't out-train a bad diet".

Far too often I've had to explain to a young man doing hours of resistance work each week who is struggling to gain size that he simply isn't eating enough, before turning around to explain to a young lady doing endless sit-ups three times a week that they won't budge her excess body fat while she's eating way more Calories than her body needs each day.

For that reason and to hit this point home, there is no exercise plan within this book. That's right, I have not included any exercise in this book. This will not only mean you can't skip straight to the exercise and ignore the nutrition, there are also three other major reasons:

1.      There is no perfect exercise plan.

1.      Exercise needs to change to ensure progression and changes to your body.

1.      Any training plan should take into account individual circumstances (work schedule/equipment available etc.).

One of the reasons people can sell training plans for 8 or 12weeks is because you cannot keep doing the same type of training for long periods of time and get results. The body adapts too quickly and then training becomes ineffective. We must change the protocols used, the exercises utilised, the repetitions, the weights used and the time rested. For example, last year, after 5 or 6months off, I rejoined the gym, for my first four weeks back I followed a simple 8-12reps of 3sets on a variety of kit changing the focussed muscles daily. After a month, I changed to supersets; putting exercises back to back to work longer and keep my heart rate up while completely fatiguing the muscles by working them to failure. After that I changed again to another programme, and so goes the cycle for 3-6weeks at a time.

## Training programmes

To allow you to change your training regularly, I have written a number of training programmes which are available via my website (SeanLerwill.com). There is a programme there for EVERYONE. The variety of different programmes allow anyone to train well thus force your body to adapt which will ensure you continue to progress and thus see results. Did I mention? There are even some FREE ones!

## I don't want to exercise

If you decide to do your own training that's fine, just remember that you MUST exercise alongside this and any REAL diet plan. Yes, you can lose body fat via nutritionally sound dieting alone, however, it won't be as long lasting and you won't look as great without exercising. You need to stimulate muscle synthesis by performing resistance (weight) training and HIIT (interval) style training. Without the training, you won't stimulate the protein synthesis needed to construct an aesthetic physique. Some people say nutrition is 70-80% of the battle, I agree to a point and used to say this myself. However, it is only true because 80% of people who get the training right (or partly right) pay no attention to diet. Diet is 70-80% of most peoples' problems. To obtain an aesthetic figure/physique diet is 50% with exercise being the other 50%.

Look at a Men's Health cover model, a Hollywood actor, a Victoria's secret model or Hollywood actress. Do you think the men obtain those pecs, delts and biceps from simply eating well? Do those girls obtain shapely legs, arms and bums from simply avoiding crisps? No. Both sets train to ensure the Calories they eat in excess (if any are excess) go to muscle formation rather than fat storage. Equally, any shapely legs or bulging biceps are a product of training that muscle group and eating the correct foods to lead to those shapely and aesthetically pleasing muscles forming. Again, without sensible nutritional choices they wouldn't be eating the right foods to ensure body changes, but without sound fitness training (that lead to a cascade of changes within the body), those nutritional choices wouldn't be half as affective.

You can see that you must train alongside a diet plan that is specific to you and your goals. That training cannot be going for a run or slow cross trainer session once or twice a week. You need to train at least three times a week, four or five times ideally. At least two or three of those sessions must be resistance/weights sessions or a session that combines resistance and cardiovascular (circuits/CrossFit style training). If you train three times a week, only one should be a run/swim/bike/cross train or yoga session. Two should be resistance based. If you train four or five times a week, then three of those should be resistance, the others LISS (light intensity steady state training - a slow run/cycle or swim) or HIIT (high intensity interval training - intervals of some kind).

To reiterate, this book is not about training. It's about nutrition and formulating a simple yet sound nutritional plan to support your goals. I just want to be clear that without a solid, progressive exercise plan to go with it, that will encourage protein synthesis, discourage muscle breakdown and encourage fat loss or muscle gain (depending on your goal) you will be short changing the fat loss or muscle building your diet plan could yield.

# Chapter 2: Nutritional Concepts

As with everything in this book, I want to try to keep it simple. Therefore, I'm am going to advocate two methods:

1.      A basic **Calorific deficit** (making sure you take in less Calories than you need) while utilising a lower-carb, moderate-fat, higher-protein diet to **lose "weight" (fat)**.

1.      A basic **Calorific surplus** (making sure you take in more Calories than you need) while utilising a moderate-carb, moderate-fat, higher-protein diet to **gain "weight" (muscle)**.

The chances are, most of you wanting to lose weight will be eating more than you need and those wanting to gain weight will be eating less than you need. Above all else when creating a diet plan **we MUST ensure that the amount of Calories you ingest is correct for your goal**. To lose fat, it needs to be less than the amount of Calories you need; not by much. Taking your Calories too low has other negative consequences that we don't want. To gain muscle, Calories ingested need to be more than the amount of Calories you need, but again, not too much or you'll gain excess body fat.

Overall however, eating a Calorific deficit or surplus is the most important part of this plan. The chances are you will have all tried a diet in the past: zone diet, Atkins diet, Paleo, carb cycling or intermittent fasting etc. The thing that each of them does (by one means or another) is to limit the amount of food you eat through a 24hour period. Some by limiting carbs, some by limiting all foods but overall the idea is to lower the amount of overall Calories you ingest. The problem arises in that everyone is different, so there really is no one size fits all. There isn't really a single "diet" that is better than all the rest as it depends on the person and what they find easier with their lifestyle and of course how/when they are training.

What do I mean by this? Well, other than lowering or raising your Calorific intake, the second most important part of any nutritional plan is whether you'll stick to it. Let's take intermittent fasting for example. If I said you can't eat until 6pm at night every day and then you have 2 meals before bed that add up to your Calorie needs for the day, that would definitely limit your ability to overeat. However, if you have client meetings all day and will be faced with bagels, croissants, sandwiches etc. the likelihood is that this plan would be very, very difficult mentally, if not impossible. Unless of course you want every meeting to start with spending 10 minutes with each client explaining why you aren't eating anything. Equally, if you are training once or twice a day, in my opinion, intermittent fasting is not ideal for a body transformation, whether trying to cut body fat or add muscle. However, it does work for some people. A colleague of mine who is a nutritionist and often on the less lean side always returns to intermittent fasting when he needs to lower his body fat. He agrees, it wouldn't work for me as well as the methods I prefer, and that's the thing: It will work for some, and not for others. Hence why you can't just copy what someone else does and expect the same results.

The take home message then (and one I want you to consider) is **compliance**. We need to create a nutritional plan that works for you: the individual. One that suits you and your lifestyle, and hence, there is no one size fits all. In short, how the nutritional plan lowers or raises your overall Calories is irrelevant; it can be by lowering carbs, cutting bread, not eating after 6pm, only eating after 6pm, eating three times a day, eating five times a day, using shakes and smoothies etc. What is relevant is that it does provide the right amount of Calories to support YOUR goal and that it does so in a way that YOU can stick to it. It's a plan that you can adhere to with YOUR lifestyle.

*Personal preference to food and diet is the number one thing that is overlooked when many are designing a nutritional programme yet is the most important thing for long term compliance and adherence.*

This book will enable you to work out how many Calories you need for YOUR goal, as well as how much protein, carbs and fats you need to support YOUR goal for your body type. But, when and how you eat them is largely up to you. I will give you what many believe is the "optimum", but above all it's what works for you with your lifestyle. If it's not practical, you won't comply and you'll give up. We don't want that. If Calories in and Calories out is of utmost importance let's concentrate on that and hope we can make that workable for you.

To make this all possible, I want to provide you with three levels of detail. What some people would term Bronze, Silver or Gold. This way, there really is something for everyone. I don't want anyone to have excuses to quit or say this isn't for them. I believe everyone should be able to at least follow the "Bronze", which will give them at a healthier and fitter existence. Silver or Gold will certainly help lead to a body transformation (either cutting fat or gaining muscle dependent on Calories) if coupled with progressive, intense training.

The three levels are:

| Level | Detail |
|---|---|
| **Bronze** | 8 Simple Rules and simple 20 Foods to Eat every day |
| **Silver** | Example Menu plans roughly based on your Calorie needs |
| **Gold** | Tracking your Calories and macros using MyFitnessPal to hit your Body Type and Goal based macros |

The first level is Bronze; simply a list of 8 Simple Rules, and then another list with 20 Foods to Eat. This gives you the simplest method and the one requiring the least amount of disruption to your life.

Silver is the Example Menus for you to follow. Silver requires a little work initially but a lot less moving forward.

Gold requires you to work out your Calories and macros and then use a smartphone app to track them daily. This requires the greatest amount of effort on your part but for many it yields the fastest and the best results.

Whichever level you think you will choose, at least read each section fully before deciding. You may be surprised by which suits you and your lifestyle best.

**BRONZE**

## 8 Simple Rules

*[handwritten: eight]*

The 8 Simple Rules are simply a group of seven ideals that if followed would likely change your health and fitness substantially. If you did nothing else from this book but take on these seven rules you would still have got your monies worth. If you also team these rules with a progressive, intense training programme then you will change your figure/physique considerably as well. There's no certainty that you will reach your "perfect" figure/physique without considering your Calorie needs, as you could still be under-eating or overeating. This is perhaps more likely to be true if you are aiming to gain muscle and therefore need to ingest more Calories. However, if you can't follow such a prescriptive plan (as laid out in the Silver or Gold areas) that sets out Calorie and macro guidelines, then embrace these seven rules and you'll be surprised what a difference they will make.

### 1.     Eat Slowly

Take your time when you eat each and every meal. This will allow you to recognise your own hunger cues. Rush your meals and your body won't have time to signal that you're eating and then that you're full. You should take at least 12-15mins to eat each meal. You should also stop when 80% full, hence why eating slowly is so important. If you eat too quickly you'll miss this cue and eat until full and most likely beyond.

### 1.     Protein

*[handwritten: search]*

You MUST eat a portion of protein with EVERY meal (Men 1-2 x palm size portions, women 1 x palm size portion). This can be fish, meat, dairy, legumes etc. If you are stuck for ideas, simply Google "protein rich foods". Simple versions in the Example Menus are tuna, chicken, cottage cheese and eggs. If you are vegetarian or vegan like me, this can be more difficult, but this is covered in more detail later. *[handwritten: will be]*

### 1.     Vegetables

Vegetables should be the main ingredients in your diet. You can prepare them any way you like; boiled; grilled; microwaved; raw; it doesn't matter. You should be eating at least 2 portions per meal. One portion being a fist sized amount. *[handwritten: two]*

Fruits are not part of this! Too many people decide they are going to be "healthy" and eat far too much fruit. Fruits are extremely nutritious; packed with vitamins and minerals, but they are also very sugary (and therefore Calorifically dense) and too easy to eat quickly and frivolously (just eat or peel and eat). Vegetables are a much better choice. Not that you can't have fruit, just ensure you have at least 4 or 5 portions of veg to every 1 portion of fruit. The vegetables you should be looking at *[handwritten: one.]* *[handwritten: four or five]*

10

are broccoli, cauliflower, spinach, pak choi, greens, kale, tomatoes among many others.

## 1. Carbohydrate

If your main aim is to lose some body fat then my experience is that for most of you (just not the skinnier person trying to add muscle), we need to get you eating less starchy carbs: pasta, bread, rice, oats etc. This is always a challenge as these tend to be the cornerstone of a western diet, hence why most westerners don't have the physiques/figures they want. A great tip is to replace these carbs with a double serving of vegetables unless this is the meal after going to the gym. After training, the carbohydrate ingested will refuel the stored energy in the muscles and aid the repair of worked muscles. If you are trying to add weight/muscle, you may well need to eat more carbs than most following the seven rules. I would therefore suggest that you do pay more attention to your Calories and macros and a tool like MyFitnessPal to log them. This is covered in far more detail later.

A good "one portion" amount for carbs is a cupped hand size amount. It's best if you can have as unprocessed versions as much as possible. Try to get foods as close to their initial state. For example potato can be baked in the skin or made into foods like Pringles. Potatoes have got a bad name over the years for making people fat; it's not the potato, it's the fact they are overeaten in processed forms like crisps and fries.

## 1. Fats

Fats have had a bad reputation, unfairly, for causing people to get fat. This is not the case, we need fats, not only for normal cell function and bodily processes, but also to help metabolise and burn body fat. You need fats from various foods to ensure you get polyunsaturated, monounsaturated and saturated fats. To do this simply eat a varied diet containing whole foods that contain healthy fats: eggs, meats, oily fish (mackerel, salmon, pilchards), olives/olive oil, nuts and seeds and spread these throughout the day.

The only caveat is a that you should avoid trans fats. These are manmade fats often as a result cooking/baking with oil that then hardens. Trans fats can be found in some processed foods such as biscuits and cakes as they were often used to help give products a longer shelf life. This isn't so common these days, but you should still avoid processed foods to be sure. Which brings us onto point six.

## 1. Avoid CRAP

Avoid processed food, or as I was once taught; C.R.A.P.

1. **C** arbonated drinks.
1. **R** defined sugar.
1. **A** rtificial colours and flavourings. (A also stands for Alcohol)
1. **P** rocessed products

By avoiding these foods, your whole body will look and feel better, not to mention run better and thus remove body fat more easily. It can be hard, but as far as possible avoid these CRAP foods. Even if you do nothing else, this change should help you live a few years extra and keep you out of the GP surgery a little more.

## 1. Drink water

Aim to drink 800ml - 1 litre for every 20kg of bodyweight. So if you weigh 55kg you should be drinking up to 2 and 3/4 litres a day. Add another litre for every hour of training.
The water will help your body function better, help it metabolise body fat as well as other body processes and help you feel fuller. People often overeat when thirsty instead of drinking. You are going to drink to make sure this isn't the case.

## 1. Sleep

Aim to sleep for at least 7 hours each night. Ideally 8 to 8 and a half hours. It might seem logical to assume that getting less sleep and therefore being awake for longer would burn more Calories (whether exercising or not) and thus in turn that would lead to more fatloss. Sadly, this is not true. Studies actually indicate that our metabolic rate is down-regulated with less sleep. When we consistently get fewer than around 8hrs sleep a night, our bodies burn Calories at a slower rate to preserve energy to help us cope with the excess rigours of longer days. Studies indicate that (on average) people burn around 400 MORE Calories by sleeping for 3 more hours each night. So don't skimp on the sleep, it'll cause your body to cope with the increased metabolic needs of longer days by sort of shifting into a lower gear, meaning the body burns fewer calories and less fat. If you are getting all the other rules right and exercising hard, you could be wasting your time if you are then not sleeping enough.
Helpful portion sizes:

| Food | Portion Size |
| --- | --- |
| **Protein** | About the size of your palm, one chicken breast, one tin of tuna or around 120-170g of food which should equate to around 20-30g of protein. |
| **Vegetables** | About the size of your fist or 1 cup. |
| **Fruit** | Half a cup or one piece. |
| **Fats** | About the size of your thumb or a golf ball (for nut butters, avocado), a tablespoon (for oils), or around 12-15 nuts. |
| **Carbs** | About the size of a cupped handful or 1/2 cup, pre-cooked (oatmeal, brown rice), or one medium sized potato. |

To reiterate:

1. **Eat Slowly** - until 80% full
2. **Protein** - with every meal
3. **Vegetables** - with every meal
4. **Carbohydrate** - reduced (unless trying to grow)
5. **Fats** - spread through the day, avoid translates
6. **Avoid CRAP** - carbonated drinks, refined sugar, artificial colours/preservatives

1. **Water** - 1litre for every 20kg bodyweight
1. **Sleep** - at least 7hrs a night. Ideally 8-8.5hrs.

## 20 Foods to Eat

*this doesn't make sense*

However you decide to split your meals, whether five meals a day, three meals a day or whatever works for you. Whether you prepare/batch cook at the weekend or prepare the night before; if you pay attention to the 8 Simple Rules while also aiming to eat as many of the foods on the 20 Foods to Eat list as you can, (within your Calories/portions) per day, you will see HUGE health, fitness and therefore most likely aesthetic changes. *by*

*or*

The 20 Foods are separated into food groups to make it easier for you to quickly know which foods are protein, which are carbohydrate and which are fats. For some of you this will be obvious and you will think it's crazy that someone wouldn't know if a food is a protein or carbohydrate. However, we all have our knowledge bases. I can go yomping (Royal Marine speak for hiking) with someone and they can name nearly every plant or flower. I haven't got a clue. A farmer can differentiate between different breeds of sheep and cattle in a second, whereas most of us simply see them as black, white, brown etc.
If you know all about carbs, protein, fats, this may be unnecessary for you, you have a skill set that makes this breakdown a little wasted. But, for those of you whose skills lie elsewhere, I'm hoping this breakdown of the 20 Foods is useful.

### Proteins

1. Lean meat (organic)
1. Salmon (not farmed where possible)
1. Eggs (free range)
1. Total Greek yoghurt (Total is my Greek yoghurt of choice, as most other Greek yoghurts have a high sugar yet low protein content. Total is the opposite; high protein, low sugar.)
1. Cottage cheese

*more fruit than veg ⇒ contradicts 3*

### Vegetables and Fruits

1. Cruciferous vegetables (broccoli, cabbage, cauliflower).
1. Tomatoes
1. Spinach
1. Berries (blueberries, raspberries, strawberries, blackberries etc)
1. Oranges
1. Bananas

*why other!*

### Other Carbohydrates

1. Whole Oats (Porridge)
1. Mixed Beans/lentils
1. Quinoa

### Good Fats

1. Raw, unsalted mixed nuts (no honey/sugar glaze etc)
1. Avocados

13

| | 1. | Extra virgin olive oil |
| | 1. | Fish oil (or algae oil) |
| | 1. | Flax seeds ground |

**Drinks / Other**

| | 1. | Green tea |

At first glance this list might seem strange. For a start, instead of "dairy", I've specifically stated Cottage Cheese and Total yoghurt. Usually you'll just see dairy written. The reason I've done this is because of the high protein content of both cottage cheese and Total (again, not any Greek yoghurt. Supermarket own versions are often high sugar and MUCH lower protein). Remember, our aim is to up the amount of protein you eat, hence these two choices.

For people out there who are vegetarian or vegan, or dairy intolerant, a good replacement for these would be coconut milk yoghurt. It is expensive, but if you want to replace things on the 20 Foods to Eat, then replacing cottage cheese and Total with coconut yoghurt is a good start.

You'll also notice that lean meat is at the top of the list, yet poultry (specifically chicken) is nowhere to be seen. My assumption is that most of us get our fair share of chicken. As a population, we completely overeat this animal. Like any thing in life, overdoing it can be bad, so try to vary your diet a little more. Red meat has got a bit of a bad reputation and some people choose to avoid it or seldom eat it. If this is for moral reasons, no problem. If not, then lean red meat is something to include in the diet, it's far better than the fast food variants many of us over- indulge in. Just don't cook it too quickly or burn it.

Finally, it might also seem strange that instead of "fish", I've gone for salmon. This is for two reasons, first if I just put fish, 90% of people would just eat tuna. It really is the chicken of the sea in that it seems to be everyone's go to fish and is again completely over eaten. Our diet is often lacking in omega 3s which are abundant in the oils in freshwater fish; hence the inclusion of salmon. The second reason I put salmon, is that it is far more likely to be found on a restaurant menu than other good oily fish like pilchards or mackerel. It is also far more socially acceptable (or so it seems) to have salmon and return to work, than mackerel or other more pungent freshwater fish.

Lastly, I haven't included protein supplements on this list, despite the fact that I used to. The reason I took it off was that people were very "Marmite" with it: they either loved the idea and overdid the use of protein supplements or hated it and because of the inclusion of protein supplements decided the whole list must be a terrible idea.

In terms of protein supplements, let's just say this (and this will be covered later in the Myths and Supplements sections); there is NOTHING wrong with protein supplements for men or women. Most protein supplements are literally just powdered milk (with the fat and sugars removed). They don't do anything other than provide protein to your body, just as yogurt, chicken or eggs do. If you are struggling to get the amount of protein you need, they are really useful. In my opinion, there is nothing wrong with including protein supplements as part of a balanced diet including the 20 Foods to Eat, but they should not be relied upon ahead of a mixed protein intake. If you are still unsure, know this; protein supplements like whey protein are very similar to other milk based powdered products like baby formula. In fact, whey protein is the main protein found in breast milk. If its good enough (and safe enough) for a baby, then you may see why its good for you!

The last thing to say about the 8 Simple Rules and 20 Foods to Eat, is that I can't take responsibility for coming up with the concept. The idea of a set of guidelines to follow daily and a set of foods to try and include came from Precision Nutrition, a company that not only helps clients with nutritional plans to support their goals, but runs courses for people like me to improve their knowledge. I had heard a lot of good things about Precision and their approach to helping people lose weight/gain muscle/improve in sports etc and hence signed up to a course after a few friends and even clients had done so. I must admit I was very impressed and also really enjoyed the course. If anyone out there finishes this book and wants to learn more, that's certainly a good place to start. source

## Plant Based Diet

For anyone who is vegan or vegetarian looking at the list of proteins thinking "well I can't eat anything", I would encourage a soy or pea based protein powder. Yes, they can taste a little strange, but either get used to it (food is fuel after all) or buy a NutriBullet and mix with spinach, berries etc so it is more palatable. The bottom line is that most vegans do struggle to get the right amount of protein to not only suit their needs but to ensure they get the whole range of amino acids (the building blocks of proteins) that the human body needs. Protein powders can really help with this. es specifically

I am vegetarian for moral reasons. I don't eat meat, but I do eat eggs, specially free range organic so I know the chickens are treated with respect. I do on occasion eat fish, but only line-caught, never farmed. We all have our moral codes and I respect that. Whether for moral reasons or health reasons, I would recommend choosing good sources of protein when you buy them. A well fed and happy chicken will produce better, more nutritious eggs. A farmed fish will not be as healthy as a line-caught and like its chicken counterpart far more likely to be pumped full of drugs and antibiotics. You want your body to be able to process foods efficiently, so don't fill it with poor quality foods.

We cover plant based diets in more detail later on. WHERE

## Precision Nutrition

I have changed the 20 Foods to Eat somewhat from the list that Precision uses for their clients, not only because I feel they are aiming at a North American audience, but because for me there were foods missing (bananas - which I think a perfect food for straight after training) which include some really important micronutrients, and foods included (BCAA powders, protein powders) that in my experience have alienated people in the past. The overall concept however, is not mine and I thank Precision for the idea and include it because I have found it very useful for helping people adapt to a healthier way of eating.

There you have it. You could stop here. You don't need to Calorie count or weigh your food if that doesn't suit you or your lifestyle. By initially getting you to choose "better" food sources, not only will you start to see changes in your health and fitness, but I bet you'll feel a whole lot better too. You'll have more energy and therefore even training becomes a fair bit easier. People often get too wrapped up in the complicated nutrition messages from various sources, when to put it simply, if you are over 20% body fat, the key is to just make the changes above outlined in the 8 Simple Rules while trying to eat the 20 Foods as much as possible.
**GOLD**

## Calories

If what is laid out above seems all well and good, but isn't quite enough for you because you like a little more detail. Or you've given it a go for a month or so, have seen some results but now need to take it further. Then now we need to talk about Calories. If you don't know, Calories or kcals refer to the amount of energy the food produces when burned in a scientific environment. In short, it's of no interest to you. What is of interest is that we can use the amount of Calories in each food to ensure you don't eat more than you need (so you don't add weight/fat) or do eat more than you need (so you can gain weight/muscle).

By creating a Calorie goal for you and specifying the amount of macronutrients (protein, carbs, fats) you can eat, we can either reduce the amount of food you are ingesting compared to what you are eating now or increase it. Either way we do so to match your goal. I would hazard a guess that in doing so, we'll be increasing the amount of protein (and possibly fats) you eat and lowering the amount of carbohydrate. This is largely because we all overeat carbs as they are so easy, cheap and readily available.

Furthermore, we have all been told for the last 20-30 years that fat is evil and causes us to be fat. This is largely misguided (see Myths section). Our bodies need fats. The only fats we should actively avoid are trans fats; the manmade fats created in some processed cakes, biscuits etc. Other fats that occur naturally are fine and have no adverse consequences if eaten as part of a balanced diet.

While we are discussing fat, what is true is that fat is more readily stored as body fat when ingested as it requires less "changing/processing" in the body. However, this will only be the case when in a Calorie surplus. Remember, overall Calorie intake is of utmost importance. This will not be the case for you if you want to lose body fat as we will ensure you are below your Calorie needs! What happens in a diet where someone isn't thinking about what they eat, is that they overheat carbs and therefore have excess Calories. This then means that excess Calories in the form of fats in the diet get stored as fat. Excess protein and carbs can also be converted and stored to fat, so eliminating fat doesn't solve that problem. Simply being sensible with the amount of Calories ingested overall is most important. **AGAIN: the amount of Calories ingested overall is most important**. Cutting out carbs, not eating carbs after 6pm, only having 2 meals a day are all irrelevant if overall Calories are still more than you need.

## Macronutrients

Calories are made up of the three macronutrients.

- Protein
- fats
- Carbs

## Protein

1. & Make you feel full.
1. • Increase your protein synthesis.
1. & Keep you anabolic (stop muscle breakdown).

As stated above, we need you to eat protein with every meal. If you are vegetarian/vegan you need to eat at least 1cup of cooked legumes/lentils with every meal or use a soy/pea/hemp etc. based protein supplement.

The RDA of protein is 0.8g/kg bodyweight. This is well under what research would indicate we really need. When training hard, we need even more protein and although not laid out in this book, we've already established that you'll be training hard. Incidentally, even if you decide not to train, don't rely on 0.8g/kg, it simply isn't enough. When trying to lose body fat we need more protein. Eating a decent amount of protein also ensures protein synthesis is switched on and remains on so we can build muscle, lower body fat and thus build a figure/physique you are proud of. To do that we simply need to ensure you are eating enough protein.

Research doesn't suggest any ill effects from eating too much protein (see Myths section). Anything you've heard about kidney problems arising from ingesting too much protein is not backed up by any research. In fact, what research does suggest is eating between 1.5-2.5g/kg of protein is required for strength/power athletes and 2-3g/kg of protein when aiming to lower body fat using a Calorie controlled diet. I would therefore say a minimum of 2g/kg and up to 3g/kg of protein is needed for anyone wanting to use my guidelines to lower their body fat or build muscle. For those that eat meat, this is far easier. For those vegetarians and vegans among you, it's a little harder, but not impossible. Hence the cup of legumes and use of vegan protein supplements mentioned before.

### Fats

As stated previously, fats have been given a really bad reputation to the point where some people still try their best to avoid them. This is fundamentally wrong. They are not to be avoided, the right fats are not only good for you but essential to a healthy, well-functioning body; and far better than bad carbs/high sugary processed foods. One of the reasons we have learned to avoid fats, is that fats are 9 Calories per gram versus only 4 Calories per gram for protein and carbohydrate respectively. While we are at it, be aware that alcohol is 7 Calories per gram!

The old thought process was to limit higher Calorie fats and therefore lower overall Calories. The problem with that is that the body needs good fats to function properly. Fats make up our cell membranes, some hormones, enable us to ingest vital fat soluble vitamins and also help in our immune systems. Ingesting fat also helps the body to utilise fat as a fuel to lower body fat.

A very low fat diet can have adverse effects on certain hormones like testosterone. Testosterone is necessary for muscle growth for both males and females. Ladies, you may be put off by the idea of wanting to keep your testosterone levels up and therefore aiding muscle growth. Don't be! Remember that growing a bit of muscle will aid fat loss and make your figure far more attractive than simply losing "weight" and looking unshapely. If you want to "tone", then you want to lose fat while "toning" (making harder) your muscles. This requires testosterone and other hormones. And of course protein (see above).

*A bad day of eating; eating well in excess of your calorie needs, especially if alcohol is involved, does not just cancel one good day. It cancels around four good days.*

## Carbohydrates

Carbs are fast becoming the new fats - the macronutrient to shun if you want to lose "weight". Yes, if we overeat a macronutrient it is likely to be carbs, but (yes I am repeating myself) it's the overall Calorie intake that is to blame, not the individual macronutrient. Therefore, don't cut out carbs completely. Rather, make sensible carb choices. Avoid high sugar versions, processed carbs and cakes/treats that mix carbs/fats together which are Calorifically dense yet nutritionally low.

Ideally you want to be eating nutritionally dense, Calorie low foods like broccoli or spinach. There's no need to avoid all breads, fruits, pastas, rice etc. Just try to choose versions of those that are closest to their natural forms. i.e. brown bread over white bread, wild rice over processed white rice, vegetables over juices. Fruits should be eaten but be aware that most are Calorie dense. Our overall concern is ensuring we don't exceed your individual Calorie needs for the day to ensure fat loss.

If aiming for muscle growth/weight gain, we need to ensure your individual Calorie needs are exceeded, but not by too much; to avoid excess fat gain as well. Any high sugar drinks, fizzy drinks, sweets etc. that have no nutritional value should be avoided. See point 6 (C.R.A.P) of the 8 Simple Rules.

*Eat with a purpose: everything that passes your lips should have a nutritional value.*

## Habits: destroying and making

There is no one size fits all or perfect eating plan. No perfect plan that works for everyone. It just doesn't work that way. As I've shown in the myths section below, it doesn't make a huge difference if you eat three meals a day or five or six, it's the total Calories that are important not how they are distributed. With that in mind, the examples Menus in the tables in subsequent pages are just ideas. They show you some of the timings and foods you could eat on various days to enable you to change your dietary habits. The meal ideas given may seem quite simple: this is because I have found that if the meals given in the examples are too complex there is a lack of compliance through either fear or complexity. Perhaps even simply being idle. This in turn causes a fall back to high street sandwich shops, thinking a bit of extra gym training or skipping breakfast might balance things out. Not the case. Unfortunately until our new habits are formed we fall back on old habits; hence we need to break the old and form the new successfully.

Humans are habitual, we get into habits and we stick to them. Most people actually buy very few items in the supermarket compared to what the supermarket stocks. We tend to find things we like and habitually buy and eat them. The same is true when visiting restaurants. One, we tend to repeat visits to one or two places we like and two, we tend to stick to the same choice; choosing safety because we are habitual. I was even told as a Marine (when looking at how you can exploit the habitual nature of humans against them) that we tend to use the same toilet cubical every time we visit a public restroom, if it's free obviously!

The problem with this habitual nature is that you need to break your bad habits before you can start new healthy ones. This is often the stumbling block. Your habits are your habits because you like those things and feel comfortable with them. To break them is in one sense going against your nature. *"No-one likes change"* said Ross in the TV series Friends and how right he was. How do we overcome our habits? We keep things simple. If the new habit is not just against your nature but also more difficult in terms of organisation and preparation, chances are you'll find a way to drift back to the old habit at some point. More often than not when tired and hungry, just when we need the new habits we are working at to be in place.

Therefore, if you are a bit of a culinary master chef, feel free to liven things up and spend more time preparing your food. Especially if it's something that will inspire you and perhaps even de-stress you. Conversely, if it's a stress and not something you enjoy then just get the basics done. I've had experience of many a person who did the basics well and then as they got into the healthy lifestyle also got into the cooking side of things and before you know it had far surpassed me and were buying cook books and sharing recipes online.

*We all have to start somewhere. But starting can lead you to amazing places. Places you perhaps never imagined.*

## Changing the way to eat

In my previous life as a Royal Marine Officer and Royal Marine PTI, undertaking physically arduous courses and tasks, I was very fit. Certainly more cardiovascular fit than I am now, but certainly not as lean. Obtaining the lean and more muscular physique I now have has allowed me to work professionally as a sports and cover model. It has allowed me to understand firsthand what is necessary to lose body fat while maintaining and even adding muscle.

The reality was that although I was incredibly fit and trained incredibly hard when I was a Commando, no amount of training was going to reveal the bottom of my six pack. No amount of sit-ups was going to make this happen. It was diet and nutrition that would do this in the end. Moreover, I learned that I could make the training I was performing even more beneficial by paying attention to my nutrition and add a little more muscle simply by ensuring my body had what it needed to repair and grow from the training I was already doing. During my time in the Marines I just ate when I ate and trained as hard as I could every time. I was fit for purpose for being a Royal Marine, but not for being a sports model! A little more (a Marinism) attention to detail (in the right place) and I turned this around.

Not convinced? Look at it this way, even if you trained for 1 hour every day, that's still only seven hours of the possible 168 hours in a week, that's 4.2%. Realistically, you'll probably be training around four or five hours per week. Perhaps you are following a programme that requires some morning running or cardio as well as evening weights session, so you are also doing three to four 15-30 minute morning LISS (low intensity steady state) cardiovascular sessions and four to five resistance training sessions of 45-60 mins per week. Still, that only equates to a maximum 7 hours , still under 5% of your time.

This means that the training you do is actually a very small percentage of the overall strategy to get you fit and healthy. Don't get me wrong, you still need to do the training. As people alway say, the changes happen outside the gym, you just spark them in it. You need to spark the body and muscles into changing and adapting to the training stimulus you provide at the gym, but then rest for the changes to take place. Beyond the training, everything else you do in those twenty three other hours a day. Or those other 160 hours per week that you're not training, can affect your goal of changing your figure/physique. From sleep, to work, to rest, to of course, food. Food is arguably the most important aspect to get right when changing your body's composition. I cannot reiterate this message hard enough!

You could say it's what this whole book is about!

## Honesty

I have tried to be as honest as possible in this book. About what I'll include. What this book was originally called. What is really necessary to change your diet and/or body. I've added in a myths section, a common mistakes section and taken the time to work out Example Menus, to try to make this workable for anyone. I am going to continue this honesty, but I want you to do the same thing for me; I want you to be honest with YOURSELF.

1.    What do you really do nutritionally?
1.    What are you really like when it comes to breaking habits?
1.    Can you really be honest with yourself?

Many reading this will be eating terribly whether you realise it or not. Your food choices will be based around fast food, supermarket lunches and supermarket deals. The majority of you will be eating way too much carbohydrate, too little protein and consider fat bad; preferring sugary treats to keep you going through the day. Let's not even start on the processed foods that probably fill cupboards and stomachs these days. And then there's alcohol.

Honesty, remember…

## Food Diary

One of the most useful things you can do is to keep a 48 hour, or even better a 7 day food diary. This is going to require complete honesty. You need to not only be completely honest and write down every biscuit, every chocolate, every spoonful of sugar in your coffee, but you also need to eat normally while you do it or it will give an unrealistic view of what you are doing. If you want to jump straight into the deep end and follow the 8 Simple Rules and 20 Foods to Eat, that's fine. But then you won't want to eat as you usually do for a few days.

However, if you do want to take a few days to see what you really do eat, it can be a worthwhile process. One that not only spells out how much you eat (or don't eat in terms of protein) but one that can even scare you into wanting to change. It can also be especially useful for you to note where your weak times of day are. Mid-morning? After dinner? Those are the habits you need to break. Change what you do at that time. Ask a partner or friend to help you avoid treats at the time. Or (and what is the most effective) empty the cupboards of the processed/sweet snacks you eat at those times. If it's there, you'll eat it. If it's not, you can't and you'll go without or choose something sensible and healthy instead.

Let's say you aren't going to do a food diary and go straight for the health trip. That's fine, commendable and understandable. However, you may miss the point of seeing how bad your previous choices were. To help, I've put together a generic breakdown of how I would suspect a large amount of people probably eat over the course of a day. I have indicated a rough amount of carbohydrate next to the foods as well as noting when macros are missing. Have a look at the foods included. You'll agree that this isn't even a particular poor day of junk food, which makes the result even more surprising.

**A typical Western diet for a day**

| Meal | Content | Comments |
|---|---|---|
| Breakfast | 1. Bowl of cereal, 50g of carbs<br>1. Milk, 12g<br>1. Banana, 24g<br>1. Tea with 1tbsp sugar and milk, 5g<br>1. **Total 91g of carbs** | **Protein:** Minimal from milk.<br><br>**Fat:** Minimal in milk but chances are it's skimmed or semi-skimmed in an old fashioned attempt to avoid fat. |
| Mid-morning | 1. Tea with 1tbsp sugar and milk, 5g of carbs<br>1. A couple of biscuits 9g/biscuit, | **Protein:** None.<br><br>**Fat:** In biscuits, so sugary/fatty biscuits which are nutritionally low yet Calorie dense. Possibly even trans fats. |

| | | |
|---|---|---|
| | 18g<br>**1. Tot<br>al 23g of<br>carbs** | |
| **Lunch** | 1. Ta<br>keaway<br>sandwich,<br>37g of carbs<br>1. Me<br>dium Apple,<br>20g of carbs<br>1. Me<br>dium<br>Orange, 15g<br>of carbs<br>1. Fru<br>it juice drink,<br>26g of carbs<br>1. Mu<br>esli Bar, 19g<br>of carbs<br>**1. Tot<br>al 117g of<br>carbs** | **Protein:** Might be some in the sandwich if lucky. However, the shop bought sandwiches will not provide the palm size amount (women) or 1-2 palm size (men) needed as protein is expensive so manufactures will limit.<br><br>**Fat:** Perhaps a little in sandwich if egg or meat or contains mayonnaise etc. |
| **Afterno<br>on** | 1. Te<br>a with 1tbsp<br>sugar and<br>milk, 5g of<br>carbs<br>1. Do<br>ughnut 26g<br>**1. Tot<br>al 31g of<br>carbs** | **Protein:** None.<br><br>**Fat:** As per biscuits, with sugary carbs in doughnut so Calorie dense, nutritionally lacking. Possibly even trans fats. |
| **Dinner** | 1. Sal<br>ad, 0g of<br>carbs<br>1. Ste<br>ak, 0g<br>1. Pa<br>sta, 30g<br>1. Bre<br>ad roll, 29g<br>1. Co<br>uple of<br>glasses of<br>wine<br>4g/glass, 8g<br>1. Ice<br>cream bar,<br>21g<br>**1. Tot<br>al 88g of<br>carbs** | **Protein:** Steak, first really good protein meal of the day.<br><br>**Fat:** Ice cream bar, but again mixed with sugar in the ice cream. |

22

| TV Snack | 1. Chocolate bar, 34g of carbs | Ch Protein: A little in the milk used for the chocolate but very minimal. Fat: From the milk in the chocolate. |
|---|---|---|

**TOTAL CARBS – 384g**

Fat: Limited and not from a variety of sources. No olive oil or olives. No nuts or nut butters. No oily fish. Limited meats. No varied dairy sources like cottage cheese or total yoghurt from the 20 Foods list.

Protein: There was one good, real protein source which was the steak. Better than nothing. If this hadn't been eaten and dinner had been a salad alone then where would protein have come from at all?

So what?

You are probably thinking: *"You said overall Calorie consumption is more important than anything else so this is just someone who eats a lot of carbs, limited protein and fats. They will probably be under Calories, so should lose weight."*

You'd think so wouldn't you? The problem is what will they lose that "weight" from? Body fat? Maybe, but often not. Muscle? Unfortunately, yes!

If they are letting their body break down its own muscle due to lack of Calories and lack of protein, they will be holding onto body fat and thus becoming a "skinny fat person". They won't be toned. They may look ok in clothes, but unclothed (or on the beach) they will feel "soft" and want to "tone". This doesn't help a person with confidence issues at all. Also, as they have allowed their body to break down its own muscle they will have lowered their own metabolism so as soon as they start to go over their Calorie needs (just add alcohol), the body fat will pile on.

As I mentioned before, if your body has carbohydrate in abundance it won't use body fat for fuel. If it has more carbohydrate than it needs (if you are in a daily Calorific surplus) then it'll store the excess carbohydrate as body fat. It doesn't matter if the excess carbs are from fruit or sweets. Though at least the fruit provides some vitamins and minerals! If it's more than your body needs, you'll put on body fat.

In the example, the person ingested 384grams of carbs in a day. Let's put that into context.

384 grams is equal to 1536 Calories. That's without including any of the protein or fats from the day's diet. You can see how easy it is to ingest too many calories. In particular, too much carbohydrate. Especially when you consider that many sources suggest an average daily Calorie intake of 1600 to 2400 Calories per day for a woman and 2000 to 3000 for a man. Some women will have almost eaten their daily Calorie allowance just from the carbohydrate they've ingested. Even a man at the top end will have eaten half his days allowance just from carbs. Now bear in mind that carbs are under half the Calories per gram of fats (4grams to 9grams). If this man ate as much fat as carbs he'd be well over his Calorie needs. It is far too easily done.

Let's look at what could be considered a better example looking at our 8 Simple Rules and 20 Foods to Eat. (Note: I'm not saying everyone SHOULD eat this way. This may suit someone trying to lose body fat for a specific Calorie goal.)

| Meal | Content | Comments |
|------|---------|----------|
| Breakfast | 1.　　3 large eggs, 2g of carbs<br>1.　　A piece of toast, 15g<br>1.　　Green tea, 0g<br>**1.　　Total 17g of carbs** | **Protein:** Good healthy portion from the eggs.<br><br>**Fat:** Great amount of healthy fat from the egg yolks. |
| Mid-morning | 1.　　Water, 0g of carbs<br>1.　　Coffee with milk, 3g<br>1.　　Almond 10-15 0.24g/nut, 3g<br>**1.　　Total 6g of carbs** | **Protein:** Protein in nuts. Not a huge amount but FAR better than cakes/biscuits.<br><br>**Fat:** Nuts are a great source of healthy fats. |
| Lunch | 1.　　Salad (2cups) with assorted vegetables (including tomatoes/carrot/peppers), 6g of carbs<br>1.　　Salmon, 0g<br>1.　　Cheese (3oz), 1g carbs<br>1.　　Water, 0g<br>**1.　　Total 7g of carbs** | **Protein:** Salmon provides a specific source of protein and the cheese provides some extra to make the palm size portion goal achievable.<br><br>**Fat:** Good saturated fats in the cheese and in the salmon. Different fats from the nuts and eggs (earlier in the day) ensuring a good daily balance. |
| Snack | 1.　　Green tea, 0g of carbs<br>1.　　Celery/carrot sticks (3 of each), 3g<br>1.　　Peanut butter (100%), 3g<br>**1.　　Total 6g of carbs** | **Protein:** As before, nuts have some protein. Not a full portion but far better choice than a doughnut or the like.<br><br>**Fat:** Nut butters (100% not those with added vegetable or palm oil) contain great healthy fats/oils. |
| Dinner | 1.　　Half a roasted chicken, 0g of carbs<br>1.　　Broccoli (2cups), 7g<br>1.　　Mixed salad (4cups), 2g<br>1.　　Peanut butter (100%) and Olive Oil Satay | **Protein:** The chicken takes care of this nicely. The peanut sauce adds a bit more to help keep portion on track.<br><br>**Fat:** Olive oil, peanut butter and some in the chicken. Again, mixed sources to ensure that 1/3 saturated, 1/3 polyunsaturated, 1/3 monounsaturated that should be aimed for. |

24

| | | |
|---|---|---|
| | Sauce, 3g<br>1.　　　Water, 0g<br>**1.　　　Total 12g<br>of carbs** | |
| **TV<br>Snack** | **1.**　　　Blueberrie<br>s 1/2 a cup, **10g of<br>carbs** | **Protein and fat:** None, but a good day overall so a snack in front of the TV packed full of nutrients. Berries are better than fruits in some ways so should be preferred as snacks go. Like nuts they are also easier to eat a few and stick to the eat until 80% full, rather than putting half a banana in the fridge. |
| **TOTAL CARBS – 58g** | | |
| A bit of a difference to the 384g we saw before. That 58g also only equals 232 Calories. Not such a dent in the day's Calorie intake, so not only far easier to get healthy fats and proteins in, but also far easier to keep to a Calorie deficit to elicit a reduction in body fat if that is the aim. | | |

I appreciate that these two days represent two completely different ends of the scale. I am not suggesting everyone needs to do the latter at all. Everyone will need different amounts of Calories and macros. In fact, if someone is wanting to gain muscle/weight, the first example with a carb amount of 384g may well be a realistic target. I would suggest better choices than biscuits, doughnuts and ice-cream bars though.

Remember, each person is different and requires a different number of Calories, fats, proteins and carbohydrates. My point is that the first example isn't that bad, no real junk food, takeaways or terrible fast foods that we know are bad. Yet the carbohydrates ramped up very quickly. Now imagine a bad day of high street takeaways, crisps, chocolate, a fast food burger and chips, a cake or bun with coffee and a few drinks at the pub after work. The Calories soon go through the roof. Consider the second example as a few simple yet sensible changes that make a real difference.

## Timing isn't everything

Although I said it doesn't matter when you eat your meals or how many meals a day you eat, as overall Calorie consumption is the most important factor. I'm going to throw one more thing at you. Actually two! There are two pieces of advice that I think, although second to overall Calorie intake, should also be considered.

There is some research to suggest that 20grams of protein every 3 hours ensure protein synthesis stays switched on in the body. This means, that eating 20 grams of protein every 3 hours will keep your body anabolic and prevent it becoming catabolic. This means it will stop your body breaking its own muscle down for fuel. This is very important not only for anyone trying to gain muscle/weight, but for anyone wanting to lower body fat. Stopping your own muscle being broken down will protect your metabolism and keep it healthy, thus allowing you to eat more Calories and avoid adding excess body fat.

Secondly, once you know your Calories needs, it can be beneficial to have a higher percentage of your daily carbs at two specific times. At breakfast (with protein as well) and after training. Our bodies are more primed to utilise carbs at these times in the ways we would like them used: for glycogen (energy store) replacement in the muscles and for general energy consumption. An added bonus is that it can also help us avoid snacking. Having said that, I'm not a fan of enforcing anything. As I said earlier, it's about compliance and that comes with what works for you. Stating "you MUST do this or that" isn't necessary or in many cases productive.

As we've already discussed, everyone is different. Being overly forceful/restrictive can hinder compliance and make you fall off the wagon so to speak. Knowing that most people either skip breakfast or just have carbs (cereal or toast), we know what we need to do. Get you eating protein with some carbs at breakfast. Overall Calories are still of most importance, so if you really can't stomach eggs on toast at breakfast, then have a protein shake and leave the carbs to be spread through the day. Remember, it has to work for YOU primarily.

## The Metabolic Meal (or MetMeal for short)

This section is specifically for those of you reading this book to lose body fat/weight and who will be eating a Calorie deficit most of the time. To give you a break from this from Calorie restriction from time to time you can use these "MetMeals". Those eating excess Calories to gain muscle/weight don't need to worry about this.

People often speak about "cheat meals", "treat meals", "free meals" or "high carb meals". They are all the same thing and to be honest, so is my "Metabolic Meal". I just think the term "Metabolic Meal" sounds a little more scientific. Added to which, this type of meal involves eating some of the things (like processed foods) that I am trying to get you to avoid in general. Due to the fact that we don't want you thinking of these foods as treats or cheats, I don't like the terms "cheat meal" or "treat meal".

In reality, they aren't a treat to your body anyway. Spinach and kale are treats to your body with a whole host of vitamins and minerals as well as fibre. Salmon treats your body to protein and omega 3 fatty acids. The types of foods you'll probably choose for your "treat/cheat" meal are in fact often quite the opposite to your body, hence I prefer to call the meals that include them Metabolic Meals. Moreover, they aren't really "cheats". I don't want you cheating on anything. This is your life. This is something that you should be trying to keep up long term. I'd rather you see it as your lifestyle with "metabolic meals" built in to allow you to fit in birthdays, weddings, work meals, date nights and just a breather from time to time.

Now I'm going to be honest. Just as I said I would be, and admit that my term is also misleading. People often speak about high carb "cheat" meals cranking up metabolism. Unfortunately that isn't very research supported. If it is the case, it's very minor. So although I have still decided to call these types of meal "metabolic meals", it's more to remind you that they are about eating higher carbs/high Calories to help keep the metabolism working, considering the rest of the time you are eating towards a Calorie deficit.

What these higher carb/Calorie meals are good for is helping normal hormonal balance (if carbs have been very low), refuelling glycogen fuel sources in the liver and muscles and most importantly for many; raising your mood and giving you something to aim for. Restricting certain foods and overall Calories can be tough at

first. You'll probably feel hungry, irritable, sluggish and maybe even a
depressed. As you get used to it and your body switches from burnin
eaten for energy to excess stored body fat for energy; your body wi'
burning machine. You'll feel fresher and more energised than ever
the processed and nutritionally empty foods and drinks avoided yc
better than you ever have before. Until you get to that point thouc
meal on the horizon can be a great place to aim for day to day, week
all need a "look forward" to keep us going from time to time, and a "MetMea
certainly play that part.

You must remember that it's important to not go way overboard in terms of Calories
during a Metabolic Meal. It's not a chance to binge on a week's worth of processed
and unhealthy foods. It's not the chance to hit up your favourite high street fast food
restaurant and order half the menu. Remember the example above when one day
added up to 1500kcal of just carbs. If your own personal Calorie needs are
1700kcal and you are eating on a deficit of 10% so 1530kcal, then you can't afford
to go completely over the top or you'll end up packing away 2500kcal. Where
possible, you should try to ensure your own maintenance Calorie (in this example
1700kcal) needs aren't exceeded while enjoying your MetMeal.

One way we do this is to make the metabolic meal a MEAL not a day. People used
to advise a cheat day, where for one day a week or every 2 weeks you can eat
whatever you want. This is not the case here. This is **ONE** meal. One sitting. Once
you leave the table, that's it. Back to the straight and narrow until the next MetMeal.
Don't go to the cinema and get coke and popcorn if you just had burger and chips
beforehand. One meal.

My advice is to enjoy a meal like a roast dinner, burger and chips, fish and chips,
pizza, spaghetti bolognese or lasagne rather than gorging on chocolate, sweets or
cakes. You can actually learn to enjoy these foods and eat some nutritious, hearty
yet Calorific meals that you may normally avoid. It's far better to do this than remind
yourself what cakes, sweets and doughnuts taste like. Not only that, the examples
I've given will likely provide the 20grams of protein whereas chocolate and cakes
won't. It's your choice, but I've found that people who move on from those things
(short of being at a birthday/wedding/Christmas and sharing in the celebrations),
tend to fare better in the long run.

## Going Old School: the Linear Diet

If you follow the 8 Simple Rules, the 20 Food to Eat and/or create a Calorific deficit
and use MyFitnessPal to monitor your intake while hitting YOUR macros, you will
lose body fat.
If you perform resistance exercise, this will happen faster (and likely be more long
lived) than if you don't. If you decide not to do resistance exercise it will be a little
slower and you won't feel as "firm" as you lose fat. Traditionally, what most people
would do (especially women) is to combine the diet plan with cardio vascular
training. Unfortunately classic cardio simply burns Calories, it doesn't help to build
muscle. What therefore happens is that they aren't building any muscle. As muscle
can help utilise Calories, without adding any, after a while their fat loss plateaus.

Our bodies crave homeostasis and adjust to the cardio training we throw at it. Our
bodies actually adjust to the lower Calories we are providing over time. This also

because working in a Calorie deficit means the body breaks down muscle
for energy when performing vast amounts of cardio with no resistance
ing to spark muscle growth/protein synthesis to ensure muscle is required and
erefore protected by the body. Our bodies "become their function". If you need
muscle because you weight train your body will hold onto it. If you do no weight
training but do lots of cardio training, your body doesn't need muscle is the same
way. Eating limited protein and a Calorie deficit means muscle will be broken down
by the body.

Over time this degradation of muscle tissue means the person doesn't need as
many Calories anymore; or has to do MORE cardio training to get the same effect
as before. The other option people tend to fall back on, is to redo the calculations to
work out their Calorie needs (from their new bodyweight) and cut Calories again.
Their weight will have dropped as they've lost weight via body fat and muscle, so
their Calorie needs will be less. On paper this seems sensible: just continue cutting
Calories until the goal is reached. At least that's the plan.

Unfortunately this rarely works long term. It is not only a huge struggle because the
body constantly tries to reach homeostasis/adapt to work with what it is given, but
as muscle is lost the person needs less and less in terms of Calories. It also often
leads to huge weight rebound when the dieter returns to more "normal" Calorie
levels. The usual is to cut and cut Calories until they feel more and more restricted.
Eating less and less so then when a holiday period or Christmas comes and they
eat more (or just more normally) they literally balloon. This is sadly often bigger
than where they started. How many times have we seen this in celebrity
magazines?

This is why it is SO important to preserve your muscle and ignore the scales.
Muscle weighs more than fat, but we WANT muscle. It not only burns more energy
than other tissue, more importantly it makes you look firm and "toned" (ladies). Not
like a walking skeleton in a bikini but like a Victoria's secret model, with curves in all
the right places. Gents, I don't need to harps on about preserving muscle. Do you
want to look like a lean muscular men's health cover model or like Christian Bale in
the Machinist? The scales are irrelevant. In most cases we don't actually want to
weight a lot less as this will mean our Calorie calculations have to go down. We
want to transform the body (lose fat and add muscle) so we **LOOK** better. The
bonus is by doing this you can look and feel better while being healthier too.

## Cardio, Cardio and More Cardio

Let's go back to the "hours of Cardio weight loss plan". As I alluded to, the human
body is highly adaptive and craves regularity/homeostasis. It therefore adapts to
any Calorie deficit over time. This means you either have to increase the amount of
exercise (think of those women you see at the gym doing 2hrs of cross trainer
every day) or lower the Calories again, and again. The body will still fight to restore
homeostasis though. In the end, the effect is that the longer someone diets and
exercises using cardio training in this manner, the harder it becomes to continue
lowering the body fat and getting the oh so sought after results. We have all seen
these people in the gym, battling with hours of cardio and eating next to nothing.
Sadly, most of these people have developed some sort of eating disorder and
probably need help getting out of the vicious cycle they are in.

28

I DON'T WANT ANYONE READING THIS BOOK TO EVER FALL INTO THAT TRAP. It is unnecessary and extremely unhealthy. It can and must be avoided at all costs.

Why? Well, one, as I've said, it's unhealthy, but secondly, although I've never been there myself, I have read and can imagine that it can make you crazy. Without getting too scientific, there is a very important hormone called leptin, which is produced less and less during dieting and restricted Calorie intake. Simply put, reduced leptin levels increase hunger and cravings while slowing the metabolic rate (meaning your body needs less Calories to function) and reducing energy expenditure. You literally crave more, but need less. All because of constant dieting. Not only is this enough to drive someone crazy, but it explains why no-one can keep this going indefinitely and why people either "bounce back" to bigger than before; eating normally but having created a body that needs less. Or develop an eating disorder and a real obsession with everything they (don't) eat.

AGAIN, PLEASE DON'T FALL INTO THIS TRAP!
To make matters worse, leptin is what we call a "master control hormone". This means its levels (high or low) have an effect on other hormones. During long periods of Calorie deficit, low leptin levels affects the levels of testosterone, growth hormone, IGF-1 and thyroid levels. Low testosterone and low GH can negatively impact not just muscle growth but libido and therefore sex lives. Women reading this probably aren't too worried right now, whereas I hope the men are won over. Gents: if you don't want your libido and muscle building affected, don't do Calorie restricted diets for long periods of time alongside vast amounts of cardio training.

For many women, I can imagine this isn't a big deal to you. Lack of muscle building and low libido probably aren't that big of a deal to you if you can feel happy and sexy with your body. What if I told you low growth hormone levels (remember GH is affected by master hormone leptin) means you'll show signs of ageing quicker: more wrinkles, thinner skin, age spots, lack of "muscle tone" and more body fat. Yes, excess Cardio and continually cutting Calories will age you more quickly.

## What's the Answer?

Continuing to cut Calories as we lose "weight" from dieting and cardio training over and over just isn't feasible long term. So what is the answer?

WEIGHT TRAINING!

As I said above, muscle weighs more than fat, it also burns more Calories than fat as a tissue. It also looks firmer and is more compact, or in fitness mag speak: it makes you look "toned". It is also far better for your heart and other organs to have lower body fat. We "simply" want to replace your body fat with a little bit of muscle.

We can't turn one into the other though! They are different. Different tissue types. It's like saying you are going to convert a steak into some butter. That's not possible. We can (through a sensible nutritional plan as outlined in this book) force your body to burn body fat and build muscle. But! We can't do this without resistance/weight training. The body needs a stimulus to build muscle and that's what resistance/weight training does.

If you do this, you may well weigh more when you step on the scales (as muscle weighs more than fat) but your waist will be far thinner, your arms have no bingo wings, your stomach, back, thighs, bum, hips have no excess fat. You may well have a six pack, especially the men. As a side, far lower body fat levels are required for women to display a six pack, which isn't always healthy. For most women this is a step too far. You can still be lean, "toned" and healthy without having washboard abs. All that this requires is that you pay attention to your nutrition and perform weight training.

In summary; if you keep continually cutting Calories and performing no exercise or just cardiovascular training to try and obtain the perfect figure or physique, you will either bounce back and re-add body fat or go crazy from food cravings, while ageing quicker and having no sex drive. To avoid this: train with weights or your bodyweight, intensely, and progressively 3-5 times a week. Thus creating some muscle and in turn losing even more body fat.

Sounds simple. That's because it is. Like the military or a science project, you just have to follow the steps. Oh, and you have to be patient.

# Chapter 3: The Nutritional Plan

The following chapter is going to help you work out your own Calorie and macronutrient requirements. If you don't want to do this yet and you want to give the 8 Simple Rules and the 20 Foods to Eat a try, that's fine. You can either read this chapter for future reference (which I recommend) or skip it for now. Whether you do or do not decide to do your calculations now, I suggest you probably will at some point in the future. This is one of the reasons why this book is a one off purchase. All you need to do is follow an intense exercise training programme (of which at least 60% of your programme is resistance/weights) for 8-12weeks and let it and the nutrition plan do its magic. At the end of the programme, re-calculate your Calorie and macronutrient needs (using this chapter) and repeat the process using a different training programme. To reiterate, I have lots of training programmes for you to follow at SeanLerwill.com.

## Maintenance Calories

The first thing we must calculate are your maintenance Calories. This is the very individual amount of Calories you need to go about your daily life. It will be slightly more if you train a few times a week, and slightly more again if you train multiple times a week or do a very active job. All you need to do is follow the guidelines below, be honest (about your weight, height and age) and let the equations do the work.

### Estimating Total Energy Expenditure (TEE)

Your "Maintenance Calorie Amount" is the Calorie intake that will match your energy expenditure (the best estimate of). If you eat this many Calories you will neither add fat/muscle or lose fat/muscle. i.e. gain weight/lose weight. Without going into too much depth, this value takes into account Total Energy Expenditure (TEE) which is made up of Resting Metabolic Rate (RMR) or Basal Metabolic Rate (BMR), Thermic Effect of Activity (TEA) and the Thermic Effect of Food (TEF).

| Acronym | Explanation |
|---|---|
| RMR/BMR | The energy required for sustaining life at rest in a fasted state (all the functions your body when resting without having ingested any food). |
| TEA | The energy required for all activity (voluntary and involuntary). |
| NEAT | Non-Exercise Activity Thermogenesis - around 15-30% of TEA is any movement that isn't really exercise like fidgeting or shivering |
| TEF | The average thermic effects of the macronutrients in digestion and is around 10-15% of TEE. |

Out of interest, the TEFs for the individual macronutrients are:

1. Protein 25-30%
1. Carbohydrate 6-8%
1. Fat 2-3%.

Another reason why a high protein diet can help with fat loss as even more energy is used just digesting it. Obviously there has to be a Calorie deficit in the first place.

The TEE is made up of the sum of RMR/BMR, TEA and TEF: you need to estimate each in order to work out your daily Calorie requirements. The best way to do this is with high tech equipment in a research facility. However, to save you hundreds of pounds we will stick to the simplest (yet still accurate) way; an equation.

There are a few different equations that have been put forward over the years. They all have their merits: some provide better results for the average person, some take account of the outsiders better than others, and some require less information so are far simpler. My preferred (and usually the most accurate - but this depends on each individual) is the Harris–Benedict equations as revised by Roza and Shizgal in 1984:

| Sex | Equation |
|---|---|
| **Men** | 88.362 + (13.397 x weight in kg) + (4.799 x height in cm) - (5.677 x age in years) |
| **Women** | 447.593 + (9.247 x weight in kg) + (3.098 x height in cm) - (4.330 x age in years) |

It looks confusing and complex, but it really isn't, so stick with me. Using some easy/average examples, let's work through the equation.

| Sex | Weight(kg) | Height(cm) | Age(yrs.) |
|---|---|---|---|
| **Male** | 85 | 182 | 35 |
| **Female** | 58 | 170 | 30 |

**Male**:        88.362 + (13.397 x 85) + (4.799 x 182) - (5.677 x 35)  =
    **1902kcal**
**Female**:      447.593 + (9.247 x 58) + (3.098 x 170) - (4.330 x 30)  =
    **1381kcal**

With the RMR/BMR calculated you now need to factor in activity (TEA) and the thermic effect of food (TEF). To do this you need to consider the frequency/intensity of your training. If you do a few easy runs/swims a week these will not be at the same level of energy needs for physical activity as intense resistance sessions or interval training. Believe it or not, activity may vary from 20% to 90% of RMR/BMR depending on the individual and what they are doing.

To make it simple, you can estimate your energy needs by multiplying your Harris-Benedict estimated RMR/BMR by an activity factor that is most applicable to your exercise routine/lifestyle:

| Activity Level | Multiplier |
|---|---|
| **Sedentary** | BMR X 1.2 (little or no exercise/desk job) |
| **Lightly active** | BMR X 1.375 (light exercise/sports 1-3 days/wk) |
| **Moderately active** | BMR X 1.55 (moderate exercise/sports/active job 3-5 days/wk) |
| **Very active** | BMR X 1.725 (hard exercise/sports/active job 6-7 days/wk) |
| **Extra active** | BMR X 1.9 (hard daily exercise/sports/physical job/2X day training) |

Let's look at the examples again:

**Male:**       RMR 1902kcal - moderately active so x 1.55 **=**       **2948kcal**
**Female:** RMR 1381kcal - lightly active so x 1.375       **=**       **1899kcal**

You may be wondering about the 10-15% for the TEF, but we take it that the activity level above takes this into account.

## Calorie Deficit / Surplus

The values above are the Calories (kcals) needed for both examples to **maintain** current bodyweight at their current activity level. However, that's not what most people want to do. People either want to **lose fat, gain muscle or both**. This means we need to lower or increase those Calories to match the person's goal. For steady controlled fat loss we can lower by 10-15%. For something a little more drastic we can lower by 20%. For muscle gain we increase by 10-20%. Any more and we'll run the risk of adding excess body fat, which unless the idea is to add body fat to be lost on something like an endurance event attempt, the majority of people don't want to do this.

Some people recommend a blanket reduction by 500 Calories for fat loss and blanket increase of 500 Calories for muscle gain. In my opinion, this is far too general. Looking at our female example above, 500kcal from her 1899 is 27%. That's a drastic reduction and something she would most definitely struggle with. Especially if she's been used to overeating at 2000kcal or more a day because she's been overdoing it. Looking at the male, 500kcal deficit from his 2948kcal would be 17%, far more manageable, but still relatively drastic. As I've said, there is no one size fits all. This goes for the diet plan and the Calorie restriction put in place.

What I would suggest here is to "Know Thyself"; something I have written about in pretty much every book I have written. We humans are actually not that self-aware, so take a minute to think about it. Are you pretty good in terms of self-control? Can you occupy your mind when hungry? Do you get angry and frustrated when hungry? Do you have friends/loved ones you live with who can help you when hungry? Will the people/person you live with entice you to eat "bad" things when hungry or will they support your goals?

Maybe ask people who know you well what they think. The reason you need to "Know Thyself" is that if you are very strong willed and mentally strong, a deficit on 20% will probably be workable for you. If you aren't, it may be too much and (going back to our compliance and adherence) will cause you to give up and fail. You don't want that. I don't want that. You therefore have to be realistic. It may better for you to reduce modestly by 10-15%. Yes, you may see slightly slower results, but at least you will stick with it, stay sane and be successful. My advice would always be to start smaller; it's a marathon not a sprint after all.
*If you have skipped forward to this section as you are off on holiday in 10 days and want a quick fix, you've come to the wrong place. Pack your Kindle/iPad etc. and read this book in full on holiday. When you come back, focus and spend 3-6 months obtaining the physique/figure you want PROPERLY. Not only will it be far more rewarding it'll last you a lifetime and be a healthy change not an unhealthy one.*

33

Not giving yourself enough time is probably the number one mistake people make. I know fitness magazines, detoxes, juice diets etc. often provide information to the contrary which doesn't help. Whatever they tell you, deciding 2 weeks before the summer holiday or big wedding that now is the time to lose 5kg is not realistic. Unfortunately, it doesn't work like that. It's highly unlikely for most people that they will be able to safely cut body fat in that short a period of time but then avoid piling it all on again afterwards. No magic diet or magic diet pill exists that can do that. The system we are working on here takes time. Ideally three months or more. Perhaps two. But this depends on the amount of body fat you want to lose. Despite the time it takes, this system will change you FOREVER so that the weight will stay off and is sustainable. That's what we all want really.

Despite the paragraph above, I have had messages from people who have used this book and gain very good and pretty fast results. For example:

*"Just thought I'd say I lost 20kg so far using the advice from your book".*

*"I was 107kg on 19/01/17, I am now 95kg (22/2/17) - and your book has been instrumental. I have every expectation of reaching my ultimate goal, and far faster than I had planned"*

All I will add is that they may have lost a significant amount of weight quickly, but they weren't planning on that. They hadn't left it until 2 weeks before a holiday. The levels of stress they were feeling compared to someone weighing themselves every hour will make a huge difference. Even more importantly, because they have lost that weight in a sensible way, albeit quickly, they have made some life changing habits which means they won't pile it back on. Instead of following a crazy, restrictive diet for a few weeks, they have removed harmful foods, increased protein intake, lowered the amount of sugar and processed foods etc and thus lost the weight naturally. They will now move forward with the same eating plan that lost them the weight and thus be healthy, happy and (as the second example intimates) where they always dreamed of being aesthetically. Remember as well that we are all different. Age, sex, sleep, lifestyle, job and of course training all play a part in weight loss. Don't be fixated on the results of these two examples, run your race and reap your rewards.

In terms of muscle gain, this is actually an even slower process. Unfortunately to add muscle naturally is a difficult process. Especially for certain somatotypes (body types). There are ways to cheat it with PEDs (Performance Enhancing Drugs), but there are drastic side effects to the body from doing so and I would therefore NEVER advise or encourage anyone to go down that route no matter how quickly they think they need results. You only get one body, it's arguably the most precious things you'll ever own. Be sensible with it and like losing body fat, give yourself time to do it safely and you'll be proud of the results. Like fatloss, we are all different so will experience muscle gain at different rates. Again, like fatloss, age, sex, sleep, lifestyle, previous training experience/previous muscle and obviously training all come into play. Just focus on your goal and don't compare with anyone else.

Back to our examples. Let's create a realistic Calorie deficit for our female and work out a Calorie surplus for our male.

To increase his Calories by 20% we multiply by 1.2. (If it was 10% it would be 1.1)

To decrease hers by 15% we multiply by 0.85. (If it was 10% it would be 0.9)

**Male:** 2948kcal x 1.2 = **3538kcal**
**Female:** 1899kcal x 0.85 = **1614kcal**

That's it. We have our Calories. They can now both use MyFitnessPal (or the like) to log EVERYTHING they eat and drink to help them track their Calories and ensure they aren't over or under by too much.

These Calorie amounts are a guide so if she ate 1596kcal that would be fine. If he ate 3480 that would be fine too. There are margins of error in the equation and the inputting of foods. For example, the human error of estimating the size of an apple. There are also the errors of average sizes and information for an egg or a slice of toast. It's all to give you an idea, and you'll be surprised how aware of what you put in your mouth it makes you by logging everything you eat.

The next stage is to use the Calorie values worked out above to provide specific macronutrient amounts based on individual sizes, needs and preferences.

## Calculating Macronutrients

As stated above, your macronutrients or macros are the amounts of protein, carbohydrate and fats that make up your Calories. Just as Calories are specific to an individual, so are the amounts of each macro. Our example males and females will have quite different amounts (perhaps not percentages) of each macro to fit their very different Calorie needs.

Before we go onto working out your macros I want to reiterate something: your total macronutrients (i.e. your total Calories) consumed is far more important for losing body fat or gaining muscle than the individual macronutrients themselves. Research also shows that glycemic index, meal frequency, type of fat, specific timing of the foods all play second fiddle to amount of Calories. They are still worth considering but ONLY when overall Calories are sorted first. If you don't ensure the right amount of Calories are ingested for YOUR goal first then macronutrient breakdown could be a waste of time. I'll say it one more time: **Calories First**!

### Somatotypes: Body Type Nutrition

Before I go into detail in this section, it's worth stating that not everyone will work this way. To be perfectly honest, for a long time, I didn't. I was far more generic. However, I now believe that there is room to be a little more specific without getting too in the weeds and making things overly complicated. After all, there is no one size fits all.

With that in mind, the next stage is to try and make your macros (from your Calorie value) a little more specific to you. There is an old, but still relevant theory called **Somatotypes** that allow us to generalise how your body is structured (thin, muscular, fat) which allows us to generalise your muscle and fat storage potential.

In turn, the macronutrient split that will best fit you and allow you to best structure your macros.

Without going into too much detail, there are three original somatotypes and two additional subsections, making five relevant somatotypes:

| Somatotype | Description |
| --- | --- |
| **Ectomorph** | Long thin muscles and limbs. Lower fat storage. Generally slim and good at endurance activities.<br><br>I would think most ectomorphs will be reading this book to GAIN size. |
| **Mesomorph** | Larger bones, solid torso, wide shoulders, trim waist and relatively controlled body fat levels. Athletic and good at sports. Often suited to bodybuilding and strength work, but equally are good at stamina and endurance.<br><br>Some want to lean up more (see abs), some want to add muscle. |
| **Endomorph** | Increased fat storage, wider waist, large bone structure. Good at strength based exercise but often hold excess fat.<br><br>Usually want to lower body fat. |
| **Ecto-Mesomorph** | Blend of ecto and mesomorph body. Athletic yet still slim, especially in the limbs.<br><br>Usually want to add muscles. Often want to lower body fat to reveal abs while adding muscle. |
| **Endo-mesomorph** | Blend between endo and mesomorph. Usually heavily muscled but with fat around the midsection.<br><br>Often want to lose excess body fat/lower body fat. |

## Somatotype Macros

The following paragraphs outline the various macro amounts for the five different somatotypes. This should hopefully allow you to pick your somatotype from the descriptions above and be specific with your macro split. In the past, I would be far more generic and then if for any reason someone wanted to take their protein consumption down, I would simply up their fats and/or carbs. Or if they wanted to decrease carbs, they may have to up fats. Calories have to come from somewhere. The problem was that people started to fiddle with macros, or asked me to do it, often based on the latest fad information. It's likely that a Google search will find someone chastising one macro or another: fat for clogging arteries and causing inflammation, protein for causing heart disease and cancer, carbs for causing diabetes and obesity. Are these things true? Partly. Are the claims supported by research? Often yes, but it's usually based on real excess of one macro or another, often in isolation.

What you have to remember, is that for every study that shows one side of the coin, there'll be another showing the other. Every study is flawed in some way, often simply in terms of human error. Of course if you feed a rat 90% red meat it'll

36

develop a disease, if you look at a human who eats processed foods, large quantities of fatty meat and dairy with very little fruits and vegetables, of course they are (likely to be) obese with heart disease and diabetes. It's all about balance and moderation. My advice is to eat every macronutrient but don't overdo any. As I said before: eat a balanced, well rounded diet, paying attention to Calories first and then (as we are doing now) a macro split to suit your body type. By using the somatotype breakdowns below, you should be able to eat the most fitting macro split to your body type which should help with your body image goal as well as your overall health and fitness.

**Protein Recommendation**

As stated previously, for a fat loss programme you need to be getting **2-3g of protein per kg of bodyweight**. Not only will this amount help you ensure muscle protein synthesis is maintained and catabolism avoided, it won't be too high as to have a negative effect on carbohydrate intake if you are playing sports (football, netball, rugby etc.) while trying to facilitate fat loss.

As stated above, protein is 4kcal per gram.

Going by our somatotypes table above, you can work out which somatotype you are and then use my advised protein value:

| Somatotype | Protein Calculation |
|---|---|
| **Ectomorph** | 2g/kgBW |
| **Mesomorph** | 2.5g/kgBW |
| **Endomorph** | 3g/kgBW |
| **Ecto-mesomorph** | 2.25g/kgBW |
| **Endo-mesomorph** | 2.75g/kgBW |

Our examples are both mesomorphs, so 2.5g/kgBW for both.

**Male at 85kg** :        85 x 2.5 = **212.5g** protein so (x4)      =
     **850kcal**
**Female at 58kg:**     58 x 2.5 = **145g** protein so (x4)      =
     **580kcal**

**Fat Recommendation**

Fat and specifically essential fatty acids, need to be ingested as they are essential for certain bodily processes to function. Certain vitamins (A, D, E, K) are fat soluble and thus enough fat must be eaten to enable the absorption of these fat soluble vitamins. Without adequate fat, these vitamins cannot be absorbed. As I've hammered home throughout this book, overall Calorie consumption is of utmost importance so fats should not be avoided. In fact, the pros (including taste and flavour to foods) that come along with eating fat can be enjoyed as long as you stay within your Calorie guidelines and try to ensure a good mix of types of fat.

Fat intake should fall between **20% and 40% of the diet**. We work this out using our Calorie value from above. I used to take a middle road with everyone to avoid complication and say 30%. This was fine and worked very well. However, the use of individual somatotypes allows us to be a little more specific to YOU and how your body may utilise fats or carbs. Hence the fat values between 20%-40%.

As stated previously, fat is 9kcal per gram.

Going by our somatotypes table above you can work out which you are, then use my advised fat value:

| Somatotype | Fat Value |
|---|---|
| **Ectomorph** | 20% of daily calories |
| **Mesomorph** | 30% of daily calories |
| **Endomorph** | 40% of daily calories |
| **Ecto-mesomorph** | 25% of daily calories |
| **Endo-mesomorph** | 35% of daily calories |

Our examples are both mesomorphs, so 30% for both.

**Male at 3538kcal:**       3538 x 0.3 = **1061kcal** so (/9)      =
    **118g**
**Female at 1614kcal:**    1614 x 0.3 = **484kcal** so (/9)      =
    **54g**

### Carbohydrate Recommendation

Once we have worked out the total Calories coming from protein and fat, we can combine them. Our carbohydrate value is then simply the remaining Calories from the Calorie value worked out initially.

Using the examples again:

**Male:**        3538kcal (total Calories) - 850kcal (protein) - 1061kcal (fats)
        = **1627kcal** which is (/4)        =
    **407grams**

**Female**: 1641kcal (total Calories) - 580kcal (protein) - 484kcal (fats)
        = **577kcal** which is (/4)        =
    **144grams**

Let's look at those macro breakdowns:

| Sex | Energy | Protein | Fat | Carbs |
|---|---|---|---|---|
| **Male** | 3538 kcal | 212.5 g (25%) | 118 g (30%) | 407 g (45%) |
| **Female** | 1641 kcal | 145 g (35%) | 54 g (30%) | 144 g (35%) |

For the male, this would seem like a relatively high carb diet considering we said earlier about how easy it is to overeat carbs. However, you have to remember that the example's goal was to **GAIN** muscle. Therefore he is on a Calorie **SURPLUS**. His fat and protein are already relatively high (although only 30% and 25% of his macros respectively) so the only place for the rest of the Calories to come from is carbohydrate. The key for this individual is what SORT of carbs. He should aim to eat non-processed, whole foods like rice, potatoes, wholemeal bread varieties, oats, quinoa, vegetables and fruits. That way he will also gain an abundance of **fibre, vitamins and minerals** which he would lack from processed Carbohydrate forms.

The female's largest macronutrient is protein, but as she is on a **fat loss** plan with a Calorie deficit, this is not a surprise. Remember we showed the energy needed to digest protein compared to the other macronutrients. She is still getting a third of her diet (give or take) from fats and from carbs respectively. Like our male "muscle gainer" above, she must endeavour to ensure her carbs are from non-processed, whole foods like starchy vegetables, grains, vegetables and fruits. Her fats should, as far as possible, be evenly split 1/3 monounsaturated, 1/3 polyunsaturated and 1/3 saturated. That way all the necessary nutrients and benefits are gained without overeating any one type and having the potential problems that are often associated with overeating saturated fats.

Following on from the above discussion about somatotypes, we can generalise the percentages of the macros for different body types. As shown below:

| Somatotype | Protein% | Fats% | Carbs% |
|---|---|---|---|
| **ectomorph** | 25 | 20 | 55 |
| **mesomorph** | 30 | 30 | 40 |
| **endomorph** | 35 | 40 | 25 |
| **ecto-mesomorph** | 27.5 | 25 | 47.5 |
| **endo-mesomorph** | 32.5 | 35 | 32.5 |

This can make things simpler if you want them to be, so instead of working out protein, then fats, then carbs, you could just work out Calories then use the percentages to give you your macros.

Let's use our examples:

Male mesomorph (muscle gain): 3538 kcal
1.      30% protein = 1061kcal = 265g protein
1.      30% fat = 1061kcal = 118g fat
1.      40% carbs = 1415kcal = 354g carbs

Female mesomorph (fatloss): 1641 kcal
1.      30% protein = 492kcal = 123g protein
1.      30% fat = 492kcal = 55g fat
1.      40% carbs = 656kcal = 164g carbs

As you can see, these values aren't the same as those worked out by specific calculations of macros. This isn't a problem though, because it highlights that overall Calories are more important than the individual Macros. Both of these strategies will work and that's the bottom line.

## Logging the macros you actually eat: **MyFitnessPal**

It's all very well working out the ideal Calories and macros to eat for your goal and body type, but if you then don't use the mathematical values at all, all the hard work was for nothing. Therefore, the last part of the process is using a Calorie counter of some sort to tot up what you are actually eating and where you can eat foods to help you hit your macros percentages.

MyFitnessPal can be simply downloaded to your Smartphone or used via the internet on a desktop computer. I won't go into any more detail as by giving it a try you can see for yourself how easy it is to use. What I will say is that it not only has a HUGE database of foods entered by people all over the world, but it also allows you to scan barcodes. If you are using a specific brand of protein powder, or just bought a big bag of oats from a supermarket; you can scan the barcode and just change your personal portion/amount of that food. Furthermore, when you enter foods, MyFitnessPal remembers them so you go to "Add Lunch" and a list of your previous entries come up. As we are all creatures of habit and so often add the same foods; this capitalises on that and makes it even easier and quicker. After a week or so, once you've added "your foods", it becomes even more useful, quick and easy.

Another huge bonus with MyFitnessPal is that you can find friends/family (or even me) on there and "friend" them. A bit like Facebook. This way, your friends can see what you are inputting and you can see what they are inputting. This can provide a support network if you struggle to stay on course. It will also ensure you fill in your MyFitnessPal daily, if that's what you've set out to do. I've used this with a number of clients in the past and found it very useful.

What's also great is that if you aren't losing body fat, you can look back and see the Calories you've been inputting and (using the pie chart/graph) what macronutrients they've come from in terms of percentages. As we know, **Calories in is THE most important part** of this, if fat loss is stalled you can choose to lower Calories ever so slightly or up the exercise, either would mean Calories in < Calories out and thus should see fat loss occur. This can work the other way as well; if you are looking to gain weight/muscles and aren't sure things are working, you can up the Calories you are eating and be sure you aren't getting things wrong by looking at your inputs for the previous weeks/months and re-assessing.

Obviously the overall success of this is down to your honesty and accuracy. If you have a sneaky chocolate bar or glass of wine it HAS to be inputted. Even if that puts you way over your Calories. Better to know today and change tomorrow than carry on over Calories and wonder why you've gained fat over 4 weeks instead of losing. To reiterate, it's really is down to honesty.

A final two points on MyFitnessPal:

### Ignore the MyFitnessPal Calorie goal for your height, weight, age

Stick with what you worked out from the formula above. Don't be lazy and just go with the value on MyFitnessPal. The likelihood is that MFP will give you quite a different amount of Calories from what we work out. MyFitnessPal's formulas will be far more generic than the ones we have used to work out your needs. The tendency therefore is to have too few Calories because MyFitnessPal's range will be far lower. Remember, if you have too few Calories the likelihood is that you'll be breaking down your own muscle. We don't want that, whatever your goal! Equally, you'll struggle to eat that little and probably get frustrated from feeling too hungry, become tired/short tempered and probably give up on obtaining the physique you want. Trust in the workings in this book, they've worked for many people, they can work for you.

### Be patient

Nothing worthwhile ever happened overnight and anything worth having is never easy. MFP will ask you how long you have to compete your goal and give you a Calorie aim for that time frame. Whether gaining or losing weight, MFP allows unrealistic timeframes as it simply uses an algorithm. Please ignore these values. Give the values we have worked out above at least 4-6weeks. If you really can't see a difference between your before and after pictures after 6weeks, then by all means lower Calories by another 5-10%.

## Using the values

Moving forward, you will take your macronutrient/Calorie values and split them over a realistic number of meals/snacks (3-6) that suits your lifestyle. I would suggest 5 small meals as this not only gives you little milestones to look forward to through the day, but also sticks with the research driven idea that 20grams of protein every three hours ensures protein/muscle synthesis is maintained and catabolism (muscle breakdown) is avoided.
But remember, the total Calories/macronutrients consumed is far more important for losing body fat than meal frequency, meal timing and even the macronutrient itself. Split your Calories across the number of meals that will work for you and your lifestyle/work commitments, try to hit the macros within them and worry about anything/everything else once those two things are sorted.

## Special cases

### Type II diabetics or insulin resistant individuals

It's best to consult your doctor or dietician before following a plan such as this. You may well need a lower carbohydrate intake. However, this would mean fats would have to increase to make up the Calories. You can see this in the thinking of the Somatotype Body Type Nutrition above; allowing for different somatotypes to have different amounts of carbs/fats. However, it is still best to consult a dietician via a GP to ensure you don't make yourself worse or put your health at even more of a risk.

### Endurance Athlete

41

If you are someone you wants to lose body fat but is training for a marathon or endurance event like a triathlon or sport like football/hockey etc, the chances are you'll feel sluggish and tired with a considerably lower carb diet. If this is the case, you can take carbs up but to ensure Calories (our overall concern remember!) stay the same you'll need to lower fats or protein to make up for the increase in carbs. The most important overall factor though, is still Calories in and out in terms of a fat loss goal. Once protein is figured out, changing carbs and fat has a small overall impact on body composition if total Calories remain the same.

## Plant Based Diet

I was vegetarian for 2 years while working in the Marines and I am most of the time again now, adding a little fish now and then. I was around 78kg and an endurance runner when a Royal Marine. I would say that carbs made up around 60% of my diet. Protein was probably only around 15-20%. I am now 83/84kg (even following a distal biceps rupture and the following recovery last year). My diet is far better suited for my goal(s) these days, even with avoiding meat. I am leaner and hold more muscle than when I was a Royal Marine. To obtain the physique I wanted, I had to change my diet, both Calories (to grow muscle) and protein content (to ensure muscle protein synthesis).

I'm not saying that those following a plant based diet can't achieve a body transformation, but it is tougher to hit the macro values, especially protein and fats when eating a plant based diet. It certainly requires more thought and more importantly, planning. I would advise utilising nuts, legumes and lentils, a pea, hemp or soy protein supplement is an absolute must and high protein carb sources like quinoa and bulger wheat will help hugely. It's also very important to eat a very varied vegetable range of veg to ensure a complete amino acid profile as well. It is possible to get all the amino acids from plants, despite what some meat eaters might say. However, no one vegetable will supply them all alone so make sure you get a variety in each and every day. If you're not vegan, I would encourage free range organic eggs as a great protein and fat source and don't worry about overeating them, see the myths section to put this to bed.

## Summary

To construct relatively accurate Calorie and macronutrient values for a fat loss or muscle gain diet, you will need to do the following:

1.      Get accurate weight and height measurements.

1.      Use the Harris-Benedict (Roza and Shizgal 1984) version for estimating RMR:

1.      **Men:**88.362 + (13.397 x weight in kg) + (4.799 x height in cm) - (5.677 x age in years)
1.      **Women:**447.593 + (9.247 x weight in kg) + (3.098 x height in cm) - (4.330 x age in years)

1.      Take the RMR value from this and multiply by an activity factor for current/ongoing activity.

1.      **Sedentary** = BMR X 1.2 (little or no exercise/desk job)
1.      **Lightly active** = BMR X 1.375 (light exercise/sports 1-3 days/wk)
1.      **Mod. active** = BMR X 1.55 (moderate exercise/sports/active job 3-5 days/wk)
1.      **Very active** = BMR X 1.725 (hard exercise/sports/active job 6-7 days/wk)
1.      **Extra active** = BMR X 1.9 (hard daily exercise/sports/physical job/2X day training)

1.      Create a Calorie deficit or surplus of between 10-20% to suit goal (fat loss or muscle gain)
1.      Protein intake between 2-3 g kg of bodyweight dependent on somatotype:

1.      **Ectomorph:** 2g/kgBW
1.      **Mesomorph**: 2.5g/kgBW
1.      **Endomorph**: 3g/kgBW
1.      **Ecto-mesomorph**: 2.25g/kgBW
1.      **Endo-mesomorph**: 2.75g/kgBW

1.      Fat intake

1.      **Ectomorph**: 20% of daily calories
1.      **Mesomorph**: 30% of daily calories
1.      **Endomorph**: 40% of daily calories
1.      **Ecto-mesomorph**: 25% of daily calories
1.      **Endo-mesomorph**: 35% of daily calories

1.      Carbs make up the rest of the Calories

1.      Remember that protein and carbs are 4kcal per gram whereas fats are 9kcal per gram.

1.      Use MyFitnessPal to log daily food intake to ensure keeping within Calorie limits set above and eating foods across a number of meals suitable for your lifestyle.

1.      Be honest!

# Chapter 4: Common Mistakes

## Cutting too many Calories

You would assume that if cutting 10-20% of your Calorie needs helps lower body fat over 8-12weeks, then cutting 40-50% will help cut body fat over 1-3weeks. No! Again: NO!

It doesn't work like that. First off all, you'll feel terrible. You'll have no energy, you'll be moody, frustrated and emotional. Worse, your body will have to get energy from somewhere. All the time we are in protein turnover, our bodies are breaking down protein and reforming it. If you are way under Calories, this broken-down protein will just as likely be used for energy as body fat. This is due to your Calories being so low. You may not think that's all bad, you'll still be losing "weight". Wrong again. You want to hang on to protein/muscle tissue at all costs, as I've said a number of times. The more muscle you have the more Calories you can eat and your figure/physique will be great to look at. DO NOT cut Calories by this much and think you'll get lean by breaking down your muscle. You'll end up eating very little Calories to maintain being that skinny, have little muscle tissue so will be a "skinny fat person" i.e. you'll be slim but will have no visible muscle tone. You'll actually have a relatively large percentage of body fat and actually be quite unhealthy. Finally, you won't be able to maintain it. You'll overeat and balloon back heavier than before just as we discussed in earlier chapters.

The same is true for gaining muscle. A surplus of 10-20% will help add muscle, yes it's slow and can seem impossible, but eating whatever you want without paying attention to Calories and eating things like ice cream and take-out burgers in an effort to have a Calorie surplus will do little more than make you fat and put you at risk from lifestyle diseases. Stick to your Calories and healthy food choices 95% of the time. Lastly, in my opinion, avoid anything that would be deemed as a PED (performance enhancing drug) to help you add muscle. The health risks are not worth it. You'll also be far more proud of your achievements and have a far more natural looking physique if you do things properly.

## Overly restrictive food choices

There are many, many diets out there that restrict the foods you can eat or give a very small list of foods you can eat. I have seen my fair share of ridiculous diet plans drawn up for people by "trainers/coaches". One example ONLY allowed white fish, chicken, broccoli and rice. The lady who had paid for this diet online from a "coach" wanted me to train her. She had spent a considerable amount of money on this "diet plan" from a "professional bodybuilder" (and an obvious PED user which I think is sadly relevant). The diet plan was totally unrealistic, but I could not convince her to give up on that diet because she had spent quite a bit of money on it and was convinced that she could obtain a physique like the "coach" who wrote it if she followed it. It was so prescriptive yet so restrictive, she was absolutely exhausted before any training took place, yet when she would discuss with the "coach" that the diet wasn't working, the coach's answer was that she must be cheating on it or eating to much. This obviously didn't help at all. Sadly, in the end I had to tell her I couldn't train her until she ditched the diet. It was so unhealthy I couldn't risk training her the way I wanted as she simply wasn't fuelled. It was sad as she wanted a "perfect" figure so much and I believe I could've helped her if only she would've eaten Calories and macros needed for HER body and goal from a wide variety of sources.

Overly restrictive or "hardcore" does not mean better results. It's not good, or healthy. Most of these very restrictive food plans (whether the designer realises it or not) aim to reduce your Calorie intake by simply making it impossible for you to overeat! I don't think anyone could overeat if only eating white fish, chicken, rice and broccoli. The problem is, that like cutting too many Calories above, most people would probably vastly under eat. Not to mention the missing fats for vitamin absorption, missing vegetable and fruit sources for actual vitamins, minerals and fibre; all affecting vital body processes. The reality is that anyone only eating white fish, chicken, rice and broccoli **WILL** fall off the wagon and run for pizza, burgers and ice cream eventually. Overly restrictive and low Calorie diets will lower the metabolism by causing the body to utilise muscle for fuel as well as affect important hormones like leptin (and due to it's master control hormone status, therefore others like testosterone and GH) and thus the bounce back and fat storage will be immense when "normal' eating is returned to, which it will have to be returned to. No-one can eat like that forever.

You don't need to be overly restrictive with the system I've outlined above. In fact, as long as it's within your Calorie allowance, you can have a little bit of dark chocolate, a latte or something else that will help you mentally on a daily basis. Just remember that of overall importance is keeping within your Calorie allowance for your goal. Beyond that, you just need to ensure you adhere to the plan for the long run. Being overly restrictive will not help with that, being a little more flexible, patient and consistent will!

## Guessing

If you've tried the 8 Simple Rules and 20 Foods to Eat and had some good advances with your figure/physique and losing body fat, you may well be wanting to take things further but on reading the section above, have reservations along the lines of: "I can't be bothered with all this maths and inputting into MyFitnessPal". I understand where you are coming from. However, I urge you to try or just stick with the 8 Simple Rules and 20 Foods to Eat. There must have been other things in your life that at first look seemed overwhelming: a work project, first day at school, moving house etc. The thing is, once we start the things we are apprehensive of, they are never as bad as we thought.

Whatever you do, don't kid yourself and guess. You won't get it right. Either do it and do it properly or don't do it at all until you can commit. Until you can commit, continue with the 8 Simple Rules and 20 Foods to Eat. When you feel you can commit, give it a go and remember that the hardest part of anything is often simply starting. So why not at least try it?

## Giving in to hunger

45

You are going to be eating less than you have been up until this point in your life. You are also going to be making far better food choices (unprocessed carbs instead of high glycemic carbs) which will help you feel fuller for longer. As will the higher protein content in your diet. So don't panic too much.

As we know from the 8 Simple Rules, one way to combat hunger is to drink more. In fact, to meet the water intake targets in this plan, you should be drinking more than you probably have before and this will hopefully help offset some of the hunger you may be worried about.

Something which I said multiple times, is that there is no one size fits all. The same is true when we are talking about avoiding hunger. Personally I like to eat 5/6 meals a day (breakfast, mid-morning, lunch, mid-afternoon, evening and pre-bed). Even when following a Calorie deficit meal plan, I still do that. I know other people who prefer 3 or 4 larger meals. As said previously, it's up to you to "Know thyself". If you are someone who can just get on with work and not feel hungry, go for 3 meals per day. If you'll get hungry due to low blood sugar and be more likely to run to the work cookie jar, then prepare your 6 meals like me and take them with you. Remember that a meal isn't necessarily a full on plate of food. A small bowl of porridge, a protein shake, a handful of nuts or a protein bar could all be a classed as a meal.

## Not training

It may seem that if you simply use the lowest activity factor, then drop your Calories by 20% you could just create an energy deficit by eating less and avoid the need to train, giving you more time to do what you like. In theory, yes this may work and I can see the draw, especially if you have a very busy work or family life, or you simply hate exercise.
In reality you will struggle to achieve the body you really want or the health benefits without training (especially with weights). Resistance training creates a cascade of hormonal changes, which you want to occur, to coax your body into holding onto muscle and utilising body fat for fuel. For men this is simpler; if you want to look like a lean muscular men's health cover model, you've got to train your muscles to build them up and keep them, while trimming the excess body fat to look lean.

For women this seems more daunting and they often doubt this idea. Instead of just relying on "dieting", perhaps throwing in some easy cardio like swimming breast stroke or reading a book on the bike or cross trainer. I understand the fear of building muscle, but you really won't build much muscle with a little resistance training while eating a Calorie deficit. What you will do, is create a body that will make you will look more like a Victoria's Secret model. All you have to do is trust me and exchange the easy cardio for some resistance training and intervals (like the training at SeanLerwill.com) and you will end up with a shapely figure with much lower body fat. More importantly, resistance training will also make the changes you make long lasting and stop you gaining weight very quickly when you go on holiday or enjoy yourself over Christmas and eat a little more.

## Not enough protein

I appreciate that throughout this book I have said that overall amount of Calories are the most important factor. I am not changing my mind, this is still the case. However, second to that I believe those that up their protein intake to the 2-3g/kg of bodyweight do far better than those that don't. I know quite a few people who have lost a vast amount of weight changing to a plant based diet. The benefits of doing this for those suffering from early onset lifestyle diseases (cardiovascular disease, type II diabetes, obesity) or a whole host of other less common conditions can be incredible; they lose a lot of weight. However, although body fat is obviously lost, muscle is also lost eating this way. What this means is that they still have a large amount of body fat, even when slim.

Most plant based eaters ingest a lot of fruit. Fruit is very nutritious (contains a lot of nutrients; vitamins and minerals) but is also very Calorie dense, meaning it contains a to of Calories. Largely because fruit contains a lot of natural sugars. This means it's actually easy to go over Calories when eating a lot of fruit. By eating a decent amount of lean, healthy choice protein while eating 1-2 portions of vegetables with each meal and keeping fruit to 1-3 pieces a day (I advise after exercise and with breakfast, rather than as easy/handy snacks through the day) a far healthier, aesthetic figure/physique is achievable.

This isn't to say you can't be a plant based diet eater and obtain a low body fat figure/physique. You just need to ensure a good helping of protein with each meal from sources you are happy to eat; be that nuts, dairy, legume/beans etc. Stick to the Calorie and macro calculations shown previously and use MyFitnessPal to hit them while sticking to a plant based diet. I do eat eggs and certainly use protein supplements to make this feasible for me, so wholeheartedly believe anyone can make a plant based idea work for them while still hitting the relevant macros.

## Bad food choices

I'm sure you're getting sick of it now, but I'm not done relating it: overall Calorie intake daily is of utmost importance. Some people take this to mean that as long as they don't go over their allowed Calories (as an example 1800kcals), they can ingest what they wish. Unfortunately this means some people spend their days eating processed fast foods, drinking wine and eating ice-cream, keeping their Calories at their threshold. Some people do this by Calories and others do it by macros, which became known as IIFYM.
IIFYM stands for "If It Fits Your Macros" is scientifically sound. Yes, if you stick to your macros and stay within Calorie allowance, you will still gain muscle or lose body fat. There's a big problem, however. If instead of the foods listed on the 20 Foods to Eat, or foods around the 8 Simple Rules, you eat ice-cream and burgers and chips (within your macro and Calorie allowances), how are you getting your vitamins and minerals in? Chances are you aren't getting enough fresh fruits and veg, and the fibre that comes along with it. Fibre is extremely important for helping rid the body of cholesterol and helping move waste through the intestines. What about good fats that help manage cholesterol? The list goes on.

Do not make this mistake. Remember that it's not just about aesthetics and looking good. You wouldn't want a Ferrari with an old rusty 1.2litre car engine in it from a banger. Your body is no different. Look after the insides not just the outside. Our bodies run far better on unprocessed natural foods, not overly processed rubbish. Using our supercar analogy again; if you spent hundreds of thousands of pounds on an Aston Martin would you fill it with knock off cheap petrol or would you pay out for super fuel? Your body is the most precious commodity you will ever have. It's still priceless! So put some decent fuel into it. It'll run better, for longer, people will pay you compliments about it and you'll have to take it into the pit for repairs far less.

## Inconsistency

I spoke to a female personal trainer and ex-dancer to get her perspective on where her friends most commonly went wrong. Her answer was inconsistency. It seems that it's common to be good and stick to the Calorie goal and training for a few days, then having a complete blow out for a day or two. Then coming back to the healthy life, then off again etc. I can see that this would fit around a Mon -Thu being good and sticking to the training and diet, then a Fri - Sun blow out that sees it all fall away. I appreciate that the thought process will be that at least 4 of the 7 days a week are on target. I'm sorry to say, it won't work.

The theory that one bad day only cancels out one good day is wrong. One bad day probably cancels up to four good days, especially if alcohol is involved. Alcohol is a poison, it is converted into acetate by the liver and acetate is then released into the blood stream where it directly inhibits fat loss. It will also lower muscle synthesis. Remember as well, that alcohol is 7kcal per gram; more than protein and carbs, so a few drinks soon adds up.

To put this into perspective:

1.      A large 250m glass of while wine is the same as one doughnut: **180 calories**.

1.      A pina colada, is the equivalent of a large cheeseburger: **450 calories**.

I am not saying do not drink. I have a collection of Scotch which I enjoy every now and then. What I am saying is that if you want to become healthier, perform better and have a body to be proud of, you need to be consistent. Going out drinking every day or even a few nights a week and overeating, but being good the rest of the time might not be enough and could leave you blaming everything but yourself for the diet and exercise plan failing. Be consistent and you'll be surprised at the results. You don't have to be completely restrictive, but have a specific limit and stick to it. It'll make letting your hair down at that wedding or on the week summer holiday all the more luxurious.

## Juice diets / detox

Much like our plant based diets, these can be good for those very close to lifestyle diseases like obesity, cardiovascular disease (heart attacks/strokes) and type II diabetes. The thing you have to ask yourself is are they realistic long term? The answer is no. No-one can eat only juice for the rest of their life. I am therefore not a fan of these "diets". Like I said before, I don't like anything that is too restrictive or prescriptive. Balance is very important and the likelihood is that if you restrict some foods in favour of others, that your body will be affected. Juice only diets fall into this exactly. Yes, a juice only diet helps someone with borderline lifestyle diseases, because it stops them eating burgers and chips, doughnuts and pasties. But so does the 8 Simple Rules and 20 Foods to Eat, but without stopping them eating nuts and other protein sources that the body needs.

Furthermore, I want to help you create something that will be long lasting and allow you to build/create a body/lifestyle to be proud of long term and therefore be healthy into your old age. These juice diets/detox diets are quick fixes; they'll help people feel better and lose a lot of weight quickly, only to see them go back to adding weight from eating "normally". It's not feasible long term. Equally, a juice diet is likely to see you fall well under your Calorie needs, and won't help you hit your macro needs either. This means you'll be well under on protein and fats. Remember we need good fats for healthy functioning of our bodies; our immune systems, cell membranes and to absorb the fat soluble vitamins that can't enter our systems any other way. Protein wise, cut protein too low and you'll breakdown your own muscle. Again, we don't want that! We need your muscle to exercise, burn more Calories and because muscles give your body a great shape so you look "toned".

I'm not saying don't drink juices at all, personally I don't. I prefer the actual fruit whole or perhaps a banana in a protein smoothie post workout. In my opinion, juices are not the best way forward but I won't chastise anyone for including them in their diet if they want to and their overall diet fits their goals, Calorie needs and macro needs. As far as juice diets go as a diet of their own, I personally wouldn't advise them.

# Chapter 5: Myths

There are a number of myths floating about in gyms, on the net and even in some fitness magazines that really don't help people make sensible informed decisions. Some people refer to these myths as "bro science". Personally I think this cheapens them a little and really just covers the more moronic suggestions like "you have to eat within 10minutes of finishing training or your workout was a waste". Other pieces of information that at first glance seem quite logical but are in fact wrong, actually often have their foundations in science. We used to think the world was flat remember, until some bright spark proved that to be incorrect. Think of these myths in the same light; it may have been thought once that to gain immortality you needed to drink what gives us life: blood. Not true and possibly the birth of vampire myths, but certainly not "bro science".

## 1.Fat makes you fat

I've already touched on this. For years people chastised fat as the cause of us all getting fat, and scientifically, that makes sense. Fat is 9kcal per gram whereas protein and carbs are 4kcal per gram respectively. The thought process was that if a macronutrient is more Calorie dense, then it would lead to more fat gain. Furthermore, being that stored adipose tissue can actually be shown to be made of the types of fats ingested (i.e. you can show the source of stored fats; polyunsaturated, even trans fats) it was assumed that ingesting fat lead to fat being stored.

As we now know, although it is easier for the body to store ingested fat as body fat than any other macronutrient, it won't do this if overall Calories are under maintenance needs. Eating fat alone doesn't make you fat, overeating makes you fat. We know that overall Calories ingested plays a more significant role than which macronutrient they are made up of. By giving a stupid example I might make this clearer. If I need 2000kcal per day, and ate 1900kcal of fat and nothing else (not realistic, but play along) I would be in a slight Calorific deficit so either stay roughly the same or slowly lose weight over time. Conversely, if I (still requiring 2000kcal per day) ingested 3000kcal of 30% protein and 65% carbs, 5% fat I would gain weight. Not slowly gain because I am eating only 5% fat, but relatively quickly because I'm eating 1/3 more Calories than I need. I don't need fat to do this. The low fat intake would not mean I can overeat, as fat is kept low, and get away with it.

These days we know a little more about the processes. Remember, we NEED fat to stay healthy. Our cells have a fat membrane and fat is integral to cells like our nerves, cells in our brains as well as for absorbing certain fat soluble vitamins. Yes, our bodies will store fat more easily as fat needs less conversion within the body to be stored, but any excess macronutrient can be converted for storage in the body.

(In theory, although the body has processes to turn excess protein into fatty acids as shown in a study by Bray GA, et al. 2012, overeating protein rather than other macronutrients can lead to increase lean mass not body fat. Let's not complicate matters though, as we are talking about fat.)

The reality is that although fat is highly Calorific at 9kcal per gram, it is necessary in a healthy diet for multiple processes in the body. Therefore, the statement that fat makes you fat is in fact a myth. Fat can make you fat if ingested in large quantities to take you above you daily Calorie needs. The real fact here is "Overeating makes you fat.

## 2.High protein intake is bad for the kidneys

In the 80s experiments were performed and showed that eating more protein increased GFR (glomerular filtration rate). The conclusion was drawn, that if GFR (the amount of blood the kidneys filtered per minute) was increased from eating more protein then the kidneys were placed under more stress from the higher workload. Therefore a high protein diet is harmful to the kidneys.

In the 90s Dutch scientists decided to look into this claim and found that while a protein-rich meal did boost GFR, it didn't have an adverse effect on overall kidney function. To date there's still no published research showing that excess protein ingestion (up to 2.8 grams per kg of body weight a day) damages healthy kidneys. The fact that no-one (bodybuilders or pro sportsmen) is likely to ingest more than 2.5-3.0 grams per kg bodyweight meaning this really covers us all.

There are other risks from overeating protein so I am not giving carte blanche to suddenly eat an 80% protein diet and become an advocate for the Atkins diet! Meat does contain saturated fats and some trans fats (not as much as processed foods, but it is still a factor if meat is overeaten). Overeating some fish can cause build ups of stored pollutants in the fish and dairy has similar issues with saturated fats and small amounts of trans fats. Meat is also quite acidic and some people suggest that high level of acidic foods could be pro inflammatory (though this is not proven) which can again occur if overeaten. Out of interest, if acidity levels are increased by some foods, it's thought we can counteract this acidity with alkaline foods, like cruciferous vegetables. Whether you choose to believe this or not, eat more vegetables!

The high protein diet myth centred on the idea that a high protein diet is bad for the kidneys, but we can see that this is not so and therefore is not something to concern yourself with. Stick to the macros you worked out, eating between 2-3kg of protein per kg of bodyweight as per your somatotype. Having said that, don't start think that as you can't really overeat protein you can't go wrong. As I've said; too much of one thing will end up being unhealthy and causing you to eat too little of something else that is necessary.

## 3.Glycemic Index awareness is essential to a healthy diet

The glycemic index was originally designed to help those with diabetes monitor how quickly a certain food source would release sugars into the blood stream. With the surge of understanding that excess carbs, in particular sugars, would lead to weight gain the glycemic index was taken up by dieters and used as the talisman of weight loss books. The idea was to avoid fast acting high sugary foods and stick to the slower release carbs. This isn't actually a bad idea on paper as it is often the highly processed and refined foods that are fast burning.

There were two major flaws with the GI diets:

1.      They put people off fruits and some other high GI foods which are essential for health and nutrients. Straight after exercise, we need higher sugary food that are high GI to refuel our glycogen energy stores. I advise my clients (and do so myself) to have a banana straight after training with a protein shake. It's THE perfect time for fruit, in particular the powerhouse of the banana.

1.      The GI value of a food changes immensely when eaten with other foods, for example a piece of fruit may be very high GI, but if eaten with fatty cheese, the cheese lowers the GI when it is being digested. Therefore, unless you are always eating foods in isolation, the GI offers nothing more than a guideline. Certainly not something to base a diet around.

A far more sensible set of rules to follow would be those laid out earlier in this book: the 8 Simple Rules and the 20 Foods to Eat. If you have knowledge of the GI system, that's not a bad thing, that information isn't wasted. In fact it can help with your post workout meal choices and general choices the rest of the time, but it should still be considered with other ideas like those presented in this book. After all, you could make a real effort with the GI and only ever eat low GI foods, but if you were over maintenance Calories what would happen? Yep, you'd gain weight. If you're only eating high GI foods, but under maintenance Calories, what would happen? Yep, you'd lose weight. Without a consideration of Calories in and Calories out, the GI is actually pretty useless on its own.

## 4.Sweet potatoes are better than white potatoes

White potatoes have got a really bad reputation in the last 5-10 years, whereas their not so distant cousin the sweet have been praised and made a meal of (excuse the pun). The real reality is, that they are actually very, very similar. White potatoes and sweet potatoes have complementary nutritional differences; one isn't better than the other:

1.      Sweet potatoes have more fibre and vitamin A.

1.      White potatoes are higher in essential minerals iron, magnesium, and potassium.

Glycemic index wise, sweet potatoes are lower on the scale, but baked white potatoes are often eaten with cheese or butter which contain fat and therefore lower the glycemic index of a meal (see above).

The question that should be on your lips, is if these potatoes are so similar why is one chastised and the other celebrated. The answer is HOW we eat them; the form in which potato is consumed. A whole baked potato is far healthier than a processed potato used to make crisps. This is far more important than the type of potato. Most people eat potatoes in the most palatable form: highly processed versions like French fries and crisps, often soaked in fat and in the years (hopefully) behind us: trans fats. Therefore the consumption of potatoes has been linked to obesity and an increased diabetes risk.

Conversely, sweet potatoes which are typically eaten whole, have been celebrated for being rich in nutrients and also having a lower glycemic index than the white variety. As we know from the paragraphs above, the GI of the potato is irrelevant on its own and without paying attention to overall Calorie intake. If you eat sweet potato fries and white potato fries, you are eating fries! If you eat a baked sweet potato you are eating a baked potato, if you eat a baked white potato you are still eating a baked potato. If you overeat while eating sweet potato anything, you are still overeating!

## 5.Eating red meat causes cancer

In the 80s a Japanese study indicated that cancer developed in rats that were fed compounds that are formed from overcooking meat in high heat. Further studies of large populations suggested a link between meat and cancer. There's a big problem with these population studies though. They rely on broad surveys of people's eating habits so they are far from conclusive. The patterns and numbers are "crunched" to find trends, not causes. Therefore it's as likely to find that cancer is caused by watching television as eating red meat.

In fact, no study has ever found a direct cause-and-effect relationship between red meat consumption and cancer. The advice from most nutritionists who still advocate meat eating (i.e. not those advocating plant based plans for moral reasons) is that you don't need to avoid burgers and steak for cancer reasons. Perhaps limit the intake so as not to overdo saturated fats from meat and if you are really concerned then order medium rare or trim off the burned or overcooked sections of the meat before eating. This is because there have been some studies towards the best way to eat meat, suggesting that the way the meat is cooked 'could' be linked to cancer if there is a link. Cooking the meat too quickly, or burning it, being the worst way to do so. There is no hard conclusive data, but if you are concerned, cook more slowly and as I said, cut away any burned bits.

## 6.5-6 small meals a day "stokes the metabolism" far more than 2-3 larger

Keeping the metabolism up is something we should try to do; it allows us to eat more Calories and thus if we want a few treats we can cope with them without suddenly adding extra pounds. As the metabolism is raised over time it allows you to ingest more Calories overall, which means you can eat more and have more wiggle room the next time you need to create a Calorie deficit for a diet before a holiday, wedding, photoshoot or the like.

However, the real way to up the metabolism is to add some muscle to your body. Muscle requires and burns more energy than other body tissue and therefore uses more Calories.

The idea that eating multiple small meals throughout the day keeps the metabolism higher isn't actually founded in truth; studies show that whether eating 2-3 meals per day or 5-6 meals a day, they have the exact same effect on total Calories burned.

53

There are benefits to eating smaller meals through the day, like preventing hunger and snacking between large meals. However, the truth still remains that there is no real effect on metabolism or the amount of Calories burned. My advice is to work out what works best for you. If eating breakfast, lunch and dinner works well around your normal western lifestyle and job, and it won't lead to you snacking on cakes or biscuits mid-morning and mid-afternoon, then go with that. If eating small meals through the day works well for you, then do that. Your overall Calorie consumption from the meals you eat (whether 3 or 6) will determine if you add or lose weight.

## 7.The body can only absorb 30g of protein at a time, any more will be stored as fat

I'm not sure where this one came from. It must be based in the theory that the human body can convert excess amino acids into fatty acids, and fatty acids can be stored as body fat. The reality is, that this is unlikely to happen (as per the Bray GA, et al. 2012 study I quoted above). What is more damning evidence that this statement is (yes I'm going to say it) "bro science" is that for excess protein to be stored as body fat it would have to be "absorbed" first. The fact that people usually say "can't be absorbed so gets used as fat" is actually factually and scientifically incorrect.

What's more impressive to me is the choice of amount: 30g. It's funny that the average chicken breast or tin of tuna is said to be around 25g of protein and most supplement brands serving is 25-30g. Could it be that this "30g absorption" value has come from people telling each other that they are wasting their money eating more/having more protein powder than the recommended serving? It could well be and in one sense people are just trying to look after each other and stop them wasting their money. If this "bro science" saves a teenager desperately wanting to add muscle from thinking "well if I double the serving, I should double my gains"; then at least it's helping!

The bottom line is that whether storing or metabolising a macronutrient, it has to be first absorbed. The body will absorb the protein, it won't just be excreted as protein. 30grams is just an arbitrary number that someone somewhere has put out there and it's stuck. I would again recommend using the macronutrient values you worked out spread across the meals you think work for you (2-3 a day up to 5-6 a day). The amount of protein at the meal is irrelevant, just the overall amount for the day and overall Calories for the day. Yes, I have stated that a study showed that 20g of protein every 3hrs can help keep protein synthesis switched on in the body. However, that is still second to overall Calories. If you aren't working with macros and are using the palm sized portion values from the 8 Simple Rules, then again, this 30g statement doesn't affect you.

## 8.Saturated fat is a major cause of heart disease

Since I was a child it has been a "known" association between saturated fats found in meats and dairy and heart disease/strokes. This was apparently particularly true

54

of red meat, butter, cakes, cream; essentially the fattier versions of those foods. The thought process being that saturated fat is believed to raise levels of low density lipoprotein (LDL) cholesterol, the so-called "bad" cholesterol, which in turn raises cardiovascular risk.

The reality is (Malhotra A. Saturated fat is not the major issue. 2013) that only one type of LDL cholesterol is associated with saturated fat intake (the large buoyant type A LDL particles). The study found that another type of LDL cholesterol (the small, dense type B particles) which are associated with carbohydrate intake, were actually linked to cardiovascular disease. They found no significant association between saturated fat intake and cardiovascular risk. Instead, saturated fat was found to be protect the heart. Dairy foods were also found to provide important dietary sources of nutrients that have beneficial effects on the cardiovascular system, such as vitamin D, calcium and phosphorus.

Another study (a 2009 meta-analysis of 26 prospective studies examining the association between total fat, fat type, and heart disease) showed that total fat intake was not significantly associated with coronary heart disease mortality or events. Actually it was found that polyunsaturated fatty-acids, those credited with being heart-healthy fats for years, recommended to reduce the risk of heart disease, were shown to be significantly associated with increased heart disease. Specifically this was Omega 6 PUFAs found in sunflower, safflower, corn, cottonseed and soybean oils. Whereas omega-3 PUFAs from fish and flaxseed were still significantly associated with decreased heart disease.

The reality is that blaming one thing for causing the lifestyle diseases such as heart disease, strokes and diabetes is probably outdated. Correlation does not mean causation. What will eventually come to fruition in my mind is that the diet WE have created in the first world of processed foods, high amounts of carb, manmade vegetable oils alongside drinking alcohol to excess and smoking, is most likely causing the diseases of today. The second issue is that we choose to medicate instead of affecting someone with exercise and diet change. Medication over diet and exercise is often just adding to the problems, if not then at least masking them.

If you want to belt and braces yourself against heart disease or strokes: avoid processed foods, don't smoke, drink sensibly and lower sugar consumption. Exercise regularly using resistance and cardio protocols with the aim of maintaining a healthy body weight/composition while eating a well-balanced diet that includes vegetables, high-quality proteins while still avoiding processed foods.

Much like the ideas laid out in this book.

Avoiding saturated fats in favour of polyunsaturated fats from questionable sources in an attempt to avoid heart disease and strokes could be doing nothing more than making the problem worse.

## 9.Egg yolks are bad for you due to high cholesterol levels

First of all if you haven't already, read point 8 above on saturated fats. Eggs were lumped into the same "dangerous foods" for heart disease. This was due to the fact that an egg yolk contains roughly 186 milligrams of cholesterol. As dietary cholesterol was thought to be the major cause of unhealthy blood cholesterol, egg yolks were scare mongered until we all only wanted to eat 1 a day or just eat egg whites.

Just like fat doesn't make you fat, cholesterol in food doesn't immediately mean high blood cholesterol. Even if it did, look at the study mentioned above in which it was shown that the saturated fat cholesterol type A isn't actually linked to heart disease, yet the type B linked to carbohydrate ingestion is. I'm not starting another war on one macronutrient or trying to start another bro-science myth. My point of view is that it's unlikely to be one causation. More likely a list of things we do in the modern world that make up a very unhealthy diet.

Whole eggs contain almost every essential vitamin and mineral we need; vitamin D, high-quality protein, omega-3 fatty acids, B vitamins and nutrients (that are ironically believed to help prevent heart disease). Most of the beneficial vitamins and minerals are found in the yolk, plus half of its protein. Eating the whites alone, which is common place amongst misguided health and fitness people, means missing out on all the vitamins and minerals as well as half the protein. Not to be forgotten as well; some additional Calories, often essential for men trying their hardest to gain muscle mass.

Perhaps one area that eggs gained their bad reputation was from their preparation and how they are eaten. It's not uncommon for eggs to be fried in butter or animal fat along with bacon and sausages. If you think about the saturated fat and cholesterol claims outlined in point 8, this makes sense along with eggs. But as I've indicated, this needn't be a real concern if you are eating a balanced diet. It goes without saying, don't eat fried eggs and bacon three times a day with no fruit of veg.

Yet again, the bottom line is that a balanced diet along the lines of the 8 Simple Rules and 20 Foods to Eat which contains eggs (whole eggs) will ensure that any food included should be fine. Dare I say it, even the odd processed product on a Metabolic Meal day?


## 10.Vegetarian and vegan diets are healthier

I've left this one to last as I didn't want to lose anyone on the way down. Let me start by saying I was a Royal Marine Commando. I always will be a Royal Marines Commando. I may not wear my Green Beret anymore, but I have a Commando dagger on my wall, two Green berets in my house and I often wear a Commando Dagger lapel badge. It's like a religion or a cult (in a good way). If someone puts the Marines down, I will stand up and protect them. They are a family to me.

Anything you feel strongly about, you will be ready to protect in a similar way, especially if it is something that is often chastised by the masses. Look at religion, when people rise against a religion, it makes those within it stick together and protect it (often without question) even more. CrossFit is the same. It gets a lot of stick (rightly at time - sorry CFers) for teaching moves far too quickly that people aren't ready for and making movements that are about lifting heavy objects, repetitive, when they really shouldn't be. However, say that to a CrossFitter and you may as well have told a Christian that Jesus is nothing more than a fairy tale.

I find the same to be true of those following a vegetarian or vegan diet. Now please remember that for 2 years while working as head of the Physical Training Department at the Commando Training Centre, I was vegetarian. Right now, I am eating a mainly vegetarian diet. I do eat eggs and dairy. When I was a Marine, I was a Quorn advocate! (Sorry). Things change and I changed. However, I know how Vegetarians and Vegans feel, especially those (like myself) who have made their choice for moral reasons. I wanted to be a vet growing up, I love animals. My father was a farmer, the manager of one of the largest farming estates in the UK, so I really do understand both sides.

Anyway, onto the subject in hand now I have given some background. Please, whether Vegan or meat eater, read on with an open mind.

When following a plant based diet, staying healthy (not fit, not aesthetic, not muscular, just healthy) completely depends on what vegetarian or vegan foods are being eaten. My first aim with any client is health. Health has to be priority. Even if the client is hell bent on aesthetics, I try to talk to them about this. Therefore, a diet of only bananas would technically be vegan, just as a diet of only dairy would technically be vegetarian. Agreed? Would either be considered healthy? No. Both would lead to serious malnutrition from missing certain macro and micronutrient (vitamins, minerals, phytochemicals) that the body needs.

Whether avoiding meat and dairy products for moral or health reasons, many plant based dieters believe that avoiding the saturated fats from meat and dairy means avoiding the supposedly adverse health effects that come with them. Another reason why I left this subject until point 10. What about points 8 and 9 above? As I've shown, much of the research stating that heart disease is down to saturated fats from meat and dairy and cholesterol from eggs is outdated and simply wrong. Therefore, a plant based diet isn't necessarily healthier for those reasons ALONE.

As I've said, I myself am vegetarian at the time of writing. My reasons being moral. If I do decide to eat meat again, I will only buy meats from a butcher where I feel the animals would've been treated humanely by having knowledge of the farm it came from prior to slaughter. At present, I have to replace my protein sources with a viable vegan and/or vegetarian alternative. Let's say someone who is obese and at risk from lifestyle diseases like diabetes and heart disease decides to take the advice of a plant based dieting dietician so drops meat and dairy in favour of more refined carbohydrates and sweets. It's obvious from what you have learned previously in this book that his/her switch to a plant based diet is not a healthy one. Perhaps a little flippant, but you see my point.

I am not trying to dissuade anyone from following a plant based diet, on the contrary. Even if you don't agree with my moral standing, as Leonardo DiCaprio point out, an estimated 14% of global greenhouse gas emissions come from the carbon emissions from the global livestock sector, with the beef and dairy industries accounting for 65% of all livestock emissions, we have to realise that as populations grow and our meat obsession does so too, our worry about greenhouse gasses has to take this into account. But I don't want this book to be about ethics and morals. The point I am making is that changing to a meat free/plant based diet requires a little more thought than no more meat or dairy. This is especially true if you want to move forward with a body transformation of losing body fat and gaining a little muscle. There needs to be a real consideration of how to obtain that palm size or so amount of protein with each meal from the 8 Simple Rules and a huge amount of consideration if trying to hit 2-3grams of protein per kg of bodyweight for somatotype structured macro amounts.

What is true and inspiring of plant based diets is how environmentally friendly they are. They are far more sustainable (and cheaper) than meat-heavy diets for the environment (as stated above in terms of Greenhouse gas emissions). Morally, when you consider that a source estimated that 21 million chickens are killed in the US a day (a day!), that figure should have an effect on you as a human being in terms of how we are abusing another species for our gluttonous needs. Again, I don't want to preach morals here.

Whatever your beliefs, vegan, vegetarian or meat eater, I hope this section has given you some food for thought (forgive the terrible pun, I thought it would lighten the mood) but if you are a plant based dieter, please do think about HOW you will eat a healthy plant based diet. Fruit alone with little or no fat or protein is not healthy.

# Chapter 6: Common Trends

The chapter on Nutrition Myths as well as my own opinion on a few different nutrition concepts and ideas throughout this book, has meant that I have touched on a few Common trends already. Whether this is cutting carbs, following the GI diet, an Atkins style plan or even the juicing trend, I hope I have made it clear that these diets work simply by cutting a macro or macros to reduce Calories, just like not eating carbs after 6pm. What's important is that we can see through these "fad" diet ideas now, as we know what they are trying to do. We know that we want to create a plan that is sustainable and healthy long term; not something that just allows you to trim some body fat without any thought of the long term health implications or sustainability. Hence, we are now going to look at a few Common Trends that you may have come across.

## IIFYM - If It Fits Your Macros

We touched on IIFYM previously. It is a popular system of eating that involves working out much of the Calorie and macro calculations we have outlined above, so you know your Calorie needs, protein, fats and carb needs and therefore can eat accordingly. The idea is that you can then eat WHATEVER you like, as long as it "fits your macros". As it says on the tin, If It Fits Your Macros allows you to do this within the remit of your "IIFYM diet plan". Due to the fact that IIFYM is actually based on science based principles, that overall Calorie consumption is of utmost importance (as we know) on paper it is a very good plan.

My personal view is that it gives people the okay to make very poor food choices because as long as their macros are hit, it doesn't matter what they eat. The argument here is that the body doesn't know the difference between one type of protein and the next, one type of carbs and the next and so on. So why pay for prime steak when you can eat cheap mince? Why worry about sweet potatoes when you can eat sweets, or if you have the macros, eat ice cream and just factor it into your fats and carb allowances. Sounds great doesn't it? Work out your macros and as long as you stick within your allocation, you can eat whatever you like day to day.

All this is great, however, when you eat rubbish there are three major things you forget:

1.      Cheap meat, cheap fish, cheap veg etc is often lower quality. So although the body may not be able to tell the difference between one type of protein and the next, what about the fact that the actual protein content is lower because the quality of the food isn't as good. Or the fact that the veg contains less nutrients and vitamins. Or the fact that the fish contains more pollutants that will enter the body. From my point of view, cheap meat also means no ethics or morals for the animal, as well as poorer quality for you.

1.      Your body may not be able to recognise protein from protein and carbs from carbs or fats from fats, but it can recognise lack of naturally occurring vitamins and minerals! Fresh fruits and vegetables will likely be missing when carb

allowances are taken up by sweets and crisps. Where are the abundance of unprocessed foods and unprocessed meats that the 8 Simple Rules would steer us to? Processed versions of meats and carbohydrates don't contain the vitamins, minerals and phytochemicals that your body needs to function correctly.

1.        Processed foods may taste good and you may be able to eat them to fill up your macro needs, but they are also often accompanied by excess salt and often chemical sweeteners. This isn't good for the body, especially when not enough fluids are ingested. Excess salt and sweeteners need more water to help process them.

In essence, I have nothing against IIFYM or people who follow it. What I would say is that like anything, if you do it to excess, it will eventually come back to bite you. IIFYM is a great way to "diet" flexibly but I would suggest it is not the way to eat every day of your life. Having said that, if you are going to eat irresponsibly IIFYM would be a better way to do it than to just gorge willy-nilly.

In my opinion, IIFYM is a great way to eat over prolonged periods of "unhealthy" eating, such as Christmas, while on holiday and the like, if you want to stay on top of things. Although, if you just want to let your hair down over those periods, then do so. If for whatever reason, you need to keep on top of the diet during more opulent periods, IIFYM can help. Personally, I think IIFYM works well if following a cycling style "diet" (see below). Using IIFYM on the high days while sticking to the 8 Simple Rules and 20 Foods to Eat on most of the other days. This way the flexibility of IIFYM can be employed every now and then. Maybe once a week, without the negatives of using it all the time.


## Carb Backloading

A few years ago the idea of carb backloading came jumping onto the scene, and again, like IIFYM the ideas behind it made sense in light of the scientific information supplied with it. This of course, made it all the more appealing to the masses. One thing I have learned in my life though, about anything really, is if it sounds too good to be true; then it often is. The idea behind carb backloading is that the body is more primed to use carbs for refuelling glycogen stores and for repair and growth post training than for conversion to fat and for storing. Therefore, eating carbs after training is most beneficial to an aesthetic figure/physique long term.

In truth, I agree with the basic sentiment alone and personally I usually have my largest carb meals post training. My evening meal and a bowl of porridge with casein/whey before bed. However, I also have porridge first thing most mornings with fruit, or eggs on some form of toast/bread. This is where carb backloading lets itself down in isolation.

First, if you train at 6pm, not having any carbs until after that time is quite hard. However, that's just the same as other diets that find a way to limit your ability to overeat through the day; hence the success some people have probably had with carb back loading. The idea that after training you can have WHATEVER carbs you want; doughnuts, pizza, burgers etc works because the rest of the day you've had none! The premise that all the carbs will be utilised for refuel and repair may sound scientifically sound, but as we know; overall Calorie consumption is of utmost important and if carb backloading means that someone who only eats carbs after training ends up under maintenance needs, they will lose weight, conversely if they eat a whole pack of donuts they are likely to end up over Calorie needs and gain weight!

If you train after work and can avoid carbs until after training, this system may well work wonders for you. However, I still have a few major issues with it. Like IIFYM, there is no real acknowledgment of vitamins, minerals or phytochemicals which our bodies NEED to function properly long term. Equally, there is no focus on macros or Calories (or at least as far as I was aware). Meaning most people using this style of eating don't seem to register the importance of overall Calorie consumption which as we know if fundamental to ANY "diet" working.

My second issue revolves around training time. What if you don't train in the afternoon or evening? What if you train at 6.30am before work? Does that mean you can then spend the rest of the day eating C.R.A.P? (see the 8 Simple Rules for this acronym) because you are "post" training all day? Without any attention to macros or Calories that could spell disaster for the 55kg woman requiring only 1600kcal to lose body fat. If after a 40min gym session at 6.30am she is then allowed to eat crisps, bread, pizza etc I hope anyone who has read this book in full can see she is likely to go over her 1600kcal goal.

My opinion (and what I personally do) is that carbs are important at breakfast; not only to fuel the day and help with concentration and energy, but to stop snacking through the day on things that will undoubtedly add up. A breakfast of eggs on toast or porridge with whey protein and fruit is not going to adversely hamper fat burning. As long as breakfast contains protein and carbohydrate and is not skipped completely, the 8 Simple Rules are followed and an overall healthy diet is being sought. Perhaps more important to point out here, is that skipping carbs in the day (until after training) is not going to increase fat burning by much at all. Research has shown little difference between fed and non-fed cardio training in the mornings. Therefore my advice is that having a decent breakfast far outweighs the protein only option.

Like IIFYM, I do think some of the ideas within carb backloading have their place. There is sense in the theory that the large carb meal post training will be utilised for refuelling glycogen stores of the body as well as being utilised for growth and repair. Most people actually fail to re-carb after training. Most people would benefit from twice as much carbohydrate as protein in their post workout shakes. Yet I am always being asked which protein supplement has the lowest carb content on the market? This is totally unnecessary. I blend my 30 or so grams of whey protein post workout with a banana and often add some dextrose or oats as well depending on the workout and the size of the banana.
I do use the carb backloading ideas myself, but not in isolation. Either as part of a carb/calorie cycling programme on my high carbs days (see below) or if I know I am going out for dinner and it is likely to be quite Calorific and carbohydrate heavy, I'll train hard an hour or so before getting ready to go out. Obviously this isn't always possible, but when it is, why not? Again, the principle itself is based in science, like IIFYM, it just shouldn't be used in isolation.

## Intermittent Fasting

Intermittent fasting is a tricky one. Personally, it's not for me, however, I have had clients who have used it to good effect. I also have a friend who is a qualified nutritionist employed by a major sports nutrition company who swears by it. As we've been coming back to again and again, there is no one size fits all. It's about Knowing Yourself and what you can make work for your mind, lifestyle and goal.

One of the major attractions with IF is that for most people it means they only have to "diet" some of the time. Either a certain number of hours a day, a few days a week or every other day, depending on the type of IF they are following. Like IIFYM and Backloading, people like this idea because it allows them to eat all the "bad" things they want to eat the rest of the time, while promising the weightloss they crave. As you've probably guessed, I don't like this approach. Where are the specific macro portions we spoke about in the 8 Simple Rules or the 20 Foods to Eat that lead us down a healthy lifestyle road and provide us with the nutrients we need (long term) for health, wellbeing and hopefully a disease free life.

It is possible to utilise IF without gorging on high Calorie, low nutrient choices. My concern is that studies have shown that when people are very hungry, they tend to reach for the sugary, fatty options first rather than the veg and quality protein, only going onto those once stuffed with the treat. It's therefore a matter of willpower, not just to fast when fasting but to eat sensibly when not.

As I explained when speaking about chastising one macro or another, or not eating carbs after 6pm, the reason these work is because they restrict Calories one way or another. IF is no different, at the end of the day, someone is restricting overall Calories. Typically, IF does this through a period of intentional Calorie restriction, there are a number of ways different IF protocols do this, a few of the common ones explained below. Some seem more difficult to manage than others and in my opinion just wouldn't be enjoyable. However, research has shown that IF in general is effective at increasing fat oxidation, reducing body weight and accelerating fat loss.

If your ears have pricked up right now, then IF might be something worth trying for you. If that's the case, you need to decide WHICH style of IF is best suited to you. Yep, time to Know Thyself. As I've said, it's not something I have tried personally, not intentionally anyway. On a few exercises during my Royal Marines career I fasted, but not out of choice. Not something I can say I relished, but I can see there are merits. Like many "diets", there are many ways to do it. I have chosen the most common, so hopefully one will fit your life style.

### Alternate Day

A very simple 24-hour rotation of low Calorie intake and normal Calorie intake, hence it's sometimes called the Up Day Down Day diet. In mice this protocol was shown to switch on the SIRT1 gene which inhibits fat storage and thus helps fat metabolism and weightloss. As I suggested above with all IF protocols, it's best to use moderation on the normal Calorie days rather than heading straight for the beer, pizza and crips.

### 5:2

The 5:2 diet is certainly one of the more mainstream IF protocols as it has hit the newspapers. One of my clients had great success with the 5:2 protocol for a period. It involves days of "modified fasting" where Calorie intake is far less than "normal" non-fasting days, either 20% of normal Calorie needs or around 400–500 Calories for women and 500–600 Calories for men. The low Calorie days are two days out of the week. The other 5 days are "normal Calories". Again, I wouldn't advise these normal days be binge days. For this to work, a sound understanding of the 8 Simple Rules and sticking to the 20 Foods to Eat could lead to some great results.

## Warrior Diet

From the title this one would make me think I should try it. Like a warrior who has been out hunting for food all day, a 20 hour fast is followed a 4 hour feeding window. The idea is that the fast will increase the actions of the Sympathetic Nervous System (fight or flight) thought to increase metabolic rate and stimulate fat metabolism. The four hours feeding time is thought to increase the activity of the Parasympathetic Nervous System and thus increase the absorption of glucose and assist with recovery from training. It would be important to ingest enough during the 4hour window to protect muscle tissue being utilised for fuel or the metabolic downshift that can occur during starvation.

## Lean Gains

I left Lean Gains until last as it seems to be one of the most common amongst people I have spoken to. I'm not sure if this is because of the name or the fact that it's a little more lifestyle achievable, as the Calorie restricted period is only 16 hours per day, 7-8 of which you should be sleeping! For many who skip breakfast anyway, this actually shouldn't be too hard. Sensibly, there's also a caveat, which is to aim for a higher protein and carb intake on training days while lowering fat, and high protein but low carb and higher fat on rest days (non training days). If I was going to give any IF protocol a go, this one sounds the most logical and doable for my lifestyle, but as we know, its about compliance and what suits you.

## Is IF for you?

If I am unlikely to ever use IF myself, then why am I putting it in my book? Well, I didn't in the first edition. But I should've done. It's so common, it deserves to be part of a current trends discussion. Equally, by giving it a place, I can explain why it works but also what could be the pitfalls. First off, as we explained with carb backloading, when given fuel (food) our bodies release insulin which brings glucose into cells to ensure energy production. Without fuel, ie. when fasting, blood glucose levels drop off drastically which in turn lowers insulin release, in turn this results in increased fatty acid oxidation. As fasting should decrease glucose and insulin levels in the body, the theory is that stored fat as will be used as the primary fuel. Sounds great doesn't it. Every great story has something though… Yep, a "but". But… studies have shown that fasting for 15-30 hours increases the rate of protein breakdown. As I've pointed out a number of times on this book, yes that might mean you'll lose weight, but not necessarily fat! You are possibly losing muscle. We want muscle to form the shapely figures/physiques people often crave but also as it's our metabolic tissue. People might say that you can offset this with supplementation with whey or BCAAs. Perhaps yes, but for me, it's not the way to do things. I don't want to have to tell people they MUST take a supplement. A supplement should never be a "must have" in my mind.

### Muscle

I would suggest that IF probably isn't the most useful way to eat if you are trying to gain muscle. If you are reading this book to gain size, and therefore need a Calorie surplus it's not something I would recommend. First off you want 20g of protein every 3hrs, you are already on a back foot with IF when it comes to that. Equally, if you have gained some size and want to cut the excess body fat off, I personally wouldn't recommend IF for the reason highlighted above; you may lose muscle. Furthermore, it's been shown that fasting for 20 hours or more lasting only two weeks, could invoke a starvation related decrease in resting metabolic rate which may slow down weight-loss. I spoke earlier about "metabolic meals" during our linear diet section, this is exactly what we don't want to happen and hence why we must have those high carb/Calorie days and is why my preferred method for cutting body fat, cycling (the next section) work so well.

### High Bodyfat Percentage

If you do have a large amount of fat to lose and think that IF may suit your needs/lifestyle, then as we said earlier, Calories in vs Calories out is the most important thing to get right. Everything (including meal timings and split) is secondary to that. I appreciate this goes slightly against what I have stated above, but bear with me. The little bit of science above suggests that fasting over 20hrs could lead to a metabolic downshift over a 2 week period. However, if you only fasted for 16hrs, this would suggest you might avoid this, therefore following a Lean Gains protocol for a while could see the benefits of IF without the pitfalls. Furthermore, something like the 5:2 or Alternate day would mean that there isn't a prolonged period of fasting as its periodic, therefore again staving off the issues explained above.

I would still suggest that for someone who is already relatively low body fat who wants to get that little bit lower, IF is not the way forward. Someone with a large amount of body fat to lose is likely to coax that away, whereas someone with relatively little is more likely to lose hard earned muscle. My advice would therefore be to steer those wanting to get rid of that last little bit to cycling. Whether someone with a lot of body fat to lose gives IF a go or goes for cycling I would leave that up to the individual and which they think will suit them best. Know Thyself remember.

## Cycling

When I was relatively fresh out of the Marines and looking at trying to lower my body fat to take my work as a sports model to the next level, I did some reading and asking around to see what worked for different people. In the end, I decided to use a style of eating called "cycling"; a process of changing the amount of a specific macro (usually carbs) and therefore Calories you eat over a series of days. People do this in all sorts of ways, from no carbs to low/medium carbs to high carbs. Most people time their low/no carb days with rest days when (in a similar

64

methodology to carb backloading and some of the IF protocols) they won't require the carbs to refuel after exercising and save their high carb days for the toughest training days like leg day or an interval session. Normal training days see a mid-range amount of carbs.

Like the IIFYM, IF and carb backloading above, cycling has its flaws and unless employed sensibly with an eye on other macros and overall Calories it won't work as well as some claim it can. If employed with an eye on the 8 Simple Rules and 20 Foods to Eat, it can be used very successfully; just like the other protocols! Personally, I have found cycling to be the easiest and most successful of all "diets", both using it myself and with many of my clients over the years.

Cycling doesn't have to be with carbs either. I've read blog posts and articles from people who cycle fats. When you cycle carbs or fats alone, without cycling others macros up or down to match the levels within Calories, you cycle Calories anyway. The useful thing about carb cycling as opposed to fat cycling is that (as I pointed out early on in this book) carbs are the macro we generally overeat simply because they are so abundant in our lives. Therefore, if you carb cycle, you can arrange your week of eating around dinners, birthdays or events so your "high carb day" falls on your major party day of the week thus helping you stay on track while still living your life. Furthermore, carbs are most useful post training as discussed previously, thus cycling carbs around our hardest training sessions ensure we get their benefits when needed, rather than avoiding completely as some inappropriate diets may advise.

I'm probably sounding like a true carb cycling convert, and in some ways I am. It is the type of "diet" I've used to get very lean, but that doesn't mean it's the one for everyone. One of the biggest mistake most bodybuilders and trainers make, is assuming that what they do will work for everyone. That isn't always the case. We are all different genetically (as we've seen from our somatotype body type nutrition section) and this requires different amounts of ratios when working out our ideal macros. To assume that just because a pro-bodybuilder (who may well be taking some form of performance enhancing drugs to help them get very lean or get very big) uses a certain diet so it will work for you, is not something you should be doing. Equally, I may find carb cycling suits me as I like to eat 5-6 meals a day so can stave off hunger with meals. Other people may eat 2-3 meals a day and therefore prefer to use Lean Gains. Each to their own.

Like IIFYM and carb backloading, you can not only use carb cycling to work around meals out and social events, but you can also step away from carb cycling at any point. When you are on holiday, relaxing during Christmas or just taking a few weeks rest, you can stop cycling and just eat "normally" (whatever that is these days) and come back to it again when that period is over. The rest from cycling can actually be a good thing. You could of course utilise one of the other protocols while stepping back from cycling, IIFYM or IF could work well when away on holiday. Or even a combination of both: sitting on the beach all day only having a few coffees and water and then eating your Calories to your macros in the evenings with friends etc at a restaurant. It's all about knowing yourself and understanding what is healthy, what is not and how Calories matter.

**High carb day**

The problem comes with cycling where people see the high carb day as a "binge" day; they've been good all week making do with little to no carbs (as they may well be taking it to an extreme instead of looking at the macros they require) so when it gets to their leg day, they do a huge leg session then hit every food group they've missed all week from pizza to chocolate to crisps to sugary cereal. The fact that this means there are periodic Calorie surpluses isn't actually a problem; giving the body excess Calories occasionally has the exact opposite effects of chronic Caloric restriction (as described above in the IF section) which is what is happening most of the time. My issue is that ideally the Calorie excess should still be from mainly good food choices to also allow an abundance of vitamins and minerals from fruits etc. which may also be restricted on low carb days.

I'm not saying no "treats"! This is still effectively one of our "Metabolic Meals", but it would be sensible to have a mix of healthy and not so healthy choices. Either way, giving the human body a one day "refeed" (I hate the term. It makes us sound like cattle, but it is essentially what we are doing) can offset the metabolic downshift that occurs with dieting that we discussed in the IF section. That desire of the body's to reach homeostasis. Not only that, the excess Calories re-boosts leptin, and thus testosterone, growth hormone, and thyroid to normal pre-diet levels. Exactly what we need to occur.

It's very simple really, but how many people do you know who do this? Think of all those very skinny women overdoing the CV and restricting their Calories more and more as each week goes by. Breaking down more muscle and doing more and more CV. If only they knew that periodic high Calorie/carb days would actually do them good. You could always recommend this book I guess? (Yes, shameless self-promotion!)

## Carb/Calorie Cycling in Practice

I think from the descriptions of IIFYM, carb back loading, IF and carb cycling you can tell I'm not really a huge fan of any of them deployed willy nilly with a blanket approach and followed without thought. I actually think all four have their merits and can be deployed, with thought, by anyone to fit certain or specific circumstances.

*My personal preference is a flexible diet (IIFYM) approach to carb/Calorie cycling with some of the considerations and ideas behind carb back loading and IF to allow someone to break away from the classic linear diet (15-20% Calorie deficit, and cut every time weightloss stalls) to ensure a healthy fat loss regime when paired with sensible training.*

If you've been dieting for a while and have simply hit a plateau, try introducing carb/Calorie cycling. It will re-sensitise your body to the fat burning and you should see a huge improvement after a few weeks. More importantly, you'll be able to employ the ideas to lose that last layer of fat that has been refusing to budge. Something introducing cycling can be very useful for.

## How to Cycle

If you still have what you consider to be a large amount of body fat to lose, it is best to ensure that the majority of the time you are in a Calorie deficit. Therefore, for all but probably four (and no more than two a week) days a month eat your base fat loss diet from the Harris-Benedict equation above with your 10-20% Calorie reduction and your specific somatotype macro values. Eat this way on both training and non-training days.

On 4-9 days a month (depending on how hard you find it to keep to the reduced Calorie and macro values) spike Calories, mainly from carbs, to maintenance levels or ever so slightly higher. Remember, your maintenance levels will be your Calories from the Harris-Benedict equation after the activity factor has been used to make it specific to your training/activity level but before you lower by a percentage to get your deficit Calorie value. When eating on your high carb/Calorie day, keep fats close to your calculated values, keep protein close to the calculated values and increase carbohydrate to make up the vast majority of the excess Calories.

This increased carbohydrates will help increase leptin levels. Carbs do this more so than good fats or protein, hence why excess Calories should be mostly carbohydrate based. The only other "rule" is that these "high carb/Calorie days" ALWAYS occur on the same day as one of your more intense (and therefore Calorie utilising) training sessions. For most people, this is a leg session (as the largest muscles in the body are in the legs), an interval (HIIT) day or an all over body day containing big compound movements of both the legs and upper body. Do not make your high carb/calorie day a rest day. Motivate yourself to train hard to earn your excess carbs and Calories!

Going back to the examples:

Remember our Female example from before? Let's go through it with her.

She had an RMR of 1381kcal and we said she was lightly active so an activity factor of x 1.375 making her maintenance Calories **1899kcal**

We wanted steady fat loss so we reduce this by 15%: 1899kcal x 0.85 **= 1614kcal**

As a mesomorph, we worked out her macros as:

1. 1641 Calories (total kcals)
1. Protein 580kcal (2.5g/kg bodyweight protein)
1. Fat 484kcal (30% Calories fats)
1. Carbs 577kcal (the rest or 35%)

For her high Calorie day, she wants to take her 1641kcal Calorie deficit figure up to her 1899kcal maintenance Calorie figure. Mostly by Carbs, meaning she will eat an extra 258kcal.

Ideally this will be 64.5grams of carbs, but it could equally be a bit of ice-cream that she usually goes without and therefore is a mix of carbs, fats and protein. She may wish to have her favourite latte from a high street coffee shop with sugary syrup. This would again be a mix of the three.

The idea is that although we would ideally want these extra carbs to be fruit or something nutrient dense, I do appreciate this is also a "treat" or reward day to keep her sane and thus having something that is usually gone without is a huge factor in keeping this working long term. Remember we discussed compliance. This is it in practice.

### Keeping it going

As your body fat lowers, you may find things start to stall or you just need to break the monotony of this regime. If this is the case, keep things exactly as above but have a high carb/Calorie day twice a week. This should still be on your leg, interval training or all over body days. You should still raising Calories to maintenance levels with increase coming mostly from carbohydrate, you are just doing so more frequently. It's still exactly the same as the example; just more frequent.

If things still don't change and the stall continues, it may be that the Calories need to be reworked. She may now weigh 55kg as opposed to 58kg, thus her Calorie and macro needs will be different. Try a couple of high carb days a week and upping the intensity of training before reworking Calories though, as ideally we want to keep the ability to utilise more Calories.

## Utilising IIFYM and Carb back loading

The main thing to remember is that you keep things normal on all days except for your high carb days. I have found that this is the simplest way to get people to utilise this type of cycling. Where possible, on a high day have the vast majority of carbs post training (carb backloading-esque) and utilise high carb days to make meals out or events more free and easy (IIFYM-esque). That way the whole process of "eating healthily" can be more appealing and more sustainable long term, rather than a 2 week juice diet that simply isn't viable with normal life long term.

The last thing I will say, is that there are many other ways to Calorie/carb cycle. Some people have no carb days on rest days, taking their Calories really low and only having carbs via cruciferous veg. Other people have very high carbs days, up to 600-700grams (depending on their size) to really "refuel". I'm not saying you should do either of these extremes, I am just giving you examples so if you come across other ideas, you are aware that they exist. I think the method I have outlined is simplest, but if you find something works better for you, go for it. At the end of the day, Calorie and carb cycling works, it doesn't seem to matter too much how you use it as long as the basic principle is adhered to and you ALWAYS remember that overall Calorie consumption is of utmost importance.

## Examples

The following examples are carb/Calorie cycling days that I have used myself or given as examples to people I've written diets for. To reiterate, just because something works for me, a sportsman, a pro bodybuilder or movie star, does not automatically mean it will work for you. This is just to give you an idea if what is written above has confused you a little.

| LOW CARB DAY | | |
|---|---|---|
| 063 0 | Pre-Breakfast | Supplements |
| | | 1. 1 x Vitamin D |
| | | 1. 1 x Fish Oil |
| | | 1. 1 x Multivitamin |
| 070 0 | Breakfast | 1. Poached eggs on steamed spinach |
| 100 0 | Mid-morning | 1. 20-30g of whey or protein blend (whey, soy, casein) |
| | | 1. Nuts (handful 10-15) |
| | | 1. Coffee (not a latte). Black. No sugar. If White (whole milk to ensure goodness in milk despite Calories) |
| 130 0 | Lunch | 1. Mackerel fillet (x1) |
| | | 1. Cottage cheese |
| | | 1. 1/2 Avocado |
| | | 1. Baked kale seasoned with cayenne pepper |
| | | 1. fresh baby spinach leaves |
| 160 0 | Mid-afternoon | 1. Chicken breast/turkey breast strips |
| | | 1. Broccoli and Cauliflower florets |
| | | 1. Guacamole |
| 200 0 | Dinner | 1. Chicken breast seasoned in chilli, ginger and olive oil |
| | | 1. Stir-fry pack with peppers, tomato, onion, broccoli and cauliflower florets cooked in coconut oil |
| | | 1. 1 x fish oil |
| 220 0 | Pre-bed | 1. Fage Total Greek yoghurt & blueberries |
| 230 0 | | 1. 1 x ZMA or Magnesium spray (e.g. BetterYou) to help sleep |

NB. Lower carb diets can affect some peoples sleep. Magnesium can help.

NB2. Fage Total Greek is given as it has the highest protein and lowest carbs of all yoghurts I've seen on the market. Don't be tempted to buy the supermarket own Greek yogurt. It may be considerably cheaper, but it tends to have half the protein and double the carbs of Total. Whether to get the 0% or 100% comes down to how many Calories a person needs. 0% if you have little Calories/fat to play with. 100% if you have more Calories/fat to get in.

NB3. Rest day, so no post workout shake.

| HIGH CARB DAY | | |
|---|---|---|
| 063 0 | Pre-Breakfast | Supplements |
| | | 1. 1 x Vitamin D |
| | | 1. 1 x Fish Oil |

| | | | |
|---|---|---|---|
| | | 1. | 1x Multivitamin |
| 0700 | Breakfast | 1. | Porridge (made with water) with 20-30g whey/blend, chopped fruit/strawberries & raspberries (or other fruit). |
| 1000 | Mid-morning | 1.<br>1.<br>1.<br>1. | Turkey strips<br>Sweet potato wedge chips (homemade)<br>Broccoli & cauliflower florets or carrot battons<br>Humous dip |
| 1300 | Lunch | 1.<br>1.<br>1.<br>1. | Salmon steak<br>Basmati rice<br>Fresh baby spinach<br>Apple |
| 1600 | Mid-afternoon | 1.<br>1.<br>1.<br>1. | Cottage cheese<br>100% peanut butter<br>Rice cakes<br>Orange |
| | Pre Workout | 1. | 20g whey or protein blend |
| | During | 1. | Water |
| | Post Workout | 1.<br>1. | 30g whey or protein blend with dextrose/maltodextrin<br>1 x large banana |
| 2000 | Dinner | 1.<br>1.<br>1.<br>1.<br>1.<br>1. | Turkey mince chilli (homemade sweet chilli sauce)<br>Sweet Potato mash<br>Kidney beans<br>Peas<br>Green beans<br>1 x fish oil |
| 2200 | Pre-bed | 1. | Porridge, Fage Total Greek yoghurt & blueberries |
| 2300 | | 1. | 1 x ZMA or Magnesium spray (eg. BetterYou) |

| MEDIUM CARB DAY | | | |
|---|---|---|---|
| 0630 | Pre-Breakfast | Supplements<br>1.<br>1.<br>1. | <br>1 x Vitamin D<br>1 x Fish Oil<br>1x Multivitamin |
| 0700 | Breakfast | 1.<br>1.<br>1. | Scrambled eggs<br>Slice of wholemeal, stoneground bread<br>Steamed spinach |
| 1000 | Mid-morning | 1.<br>1.<br>1. | Chicken breast<br>Celery sticks<br>100% nut butter |
| 1300 | Lunch | 1.<br>1.<br>1.<br>1.<br>1. | Salmon steak<br>Baked sweet potato<br>Baked kale<br>1/2 Avocado<br>1 x fish oil |
| 1600 | Mid afternoon | 1.<br>1. | Cottage cheese<br>Rice cakes |

70

| | | | |
|---|---|---|---|
| | | 1. | Apple |
| | **Pre Workout** | 1. | 20g whey or protein blend |
| | **During** | 1. | Water |
| | **Post Workout** | 1. | 30g whey or protein blend |
| | | 1. | 1 x banana |
| 2000 | **Dinner** | 1. | Tuna (spring water) |
| | | 1. | Quinoa |
| | | 1. | Broccoli |
| | | 1. | Cauliflower |
| | | 1. | Mixed beans/pulses |
| | | 1. | Chillies |
| | | 1. | 1 x fish oil |
| 2200 | **Pre-bed** | 1. | Porridge, Fage Total Greek yoghurt & blackberries |
| 2300 | | 1. | 1 x ZMA or Magnesium spray (eg. BetterYou) |

NB. To reiterate, these are examples that I have either used myself or given to other people. They are simple and easy to ensure compliance. The macro and Calorie amounts depend on the person and can be worked out and hit while keeping to the kinds of foods listed. They aren't to be followed, they are to give an idea.

# Chapter 7: Example Menus

We human beings loves examples. When I was being taught how to teach in the Royal Marines we used the acronym EDIP - Explanation, Demonstration, Imitation, Practice. We need the *demonstration* to best suit those visual learners as opposed to the auditory learners. In reality though we all like a good example or best example of how to do things, and that's what these examples are for.

We know from the information in the previous chapters that one Example Menu isn't going to be suitable for everyone. We have different Calorie needs, different macro needs and we all (ideally) like to eat in slightly different ways. Obviously, like any example, it has to cater for the mean (average) person; it has to be suited to more people than not. That is what I've tried to create here.

When looking at creating my own nutrition guide (about 4 years ago) I came up with the idea of the "Ration Pack Diet". A diet plan that like a Ration Pack provides you with everything you need for 24hrs; just like a solider being handed a cardboard box with his rations for 24hrs. The tricky part of this that most non-military people won't enjoy, and to be honest soldiers aren't too keen on, is that sometimes you end up eating the same thing day after day! I've often spoken to friends in the Marines who have stated that they had the same ration pack for many, many, many days in a row. The idea is that you get different menus from day to day, so that breakfast ranges from bacon and beans, to sausage and beans, burger and beans etc. Evening meals range from lamb stew, to pork casserole, to chicken pasta. However, we've all found ourselves on an exercise or operations where you are presented with the same pack for a considerable amount of time; the same breakfast, the same evening meal, the pudding. It happens.

To a soldier, food is fuel, and you are so hungry you don't care (too much) that it's the same. No-one leaves it! With this in mind, I decided to create a book that gave the same thing: simple Ration Pack style menus that were as simple as possible; my aim was to make this something people could realistically and simply recreate.

What I found was that from these humble beginnings, my book became so much more than simple Ration Pack plans; it became a complete guide to eating healthily and hence it became "The Complete Guide to Successful Eating". My aim now being to help people navigate the over abundance of good (and bad) information and enable them to create a nutritional plan that was simple, suitable for their goals and above all easy for their lifestyle. Although "The Ration Pack Diet" did this, it didn't seem to tell people it was going to do this. Hence in this book the Ration Pack section is now simply an Example Menu chapter rather than the Ration Packs themselves.

Prior to this chapter, you've had two other options for your nutrition plan:

1.      The 8 Simple Rules and the 20 Foods to Eat. Use these two ideas and you will eat more healthily, changing your health and your fitness and in turn your physique/figure.

1.      Your Calories, your macros specific to your somatotype and your goal; whether that be to lose fat or gain muscle. Calorie/Carb cycling to utilise if this will help you take the process even further. All these options require MyFitnessPal to monitor what you are eating.

These Example Menus are meant to give you another option; in some ways the easiest of all. You don't need to worry about MyFitnessPal or checking the 20 Foods to Eat or 8 Simple Rules. All you have to do is work out your Calorie needs using the Harris-Benedict equation in previous chapters, multiply by an activity factor, lower or increase by 10-20% to make a Calorific deficit or surplus depending on whether you want to add muscle or lose fat respectively and then choose the Example Menu below, closest to your Calorie number needs. Choose the Example Menu just above your personal figure if you are trying to gain muscle and just below, if trying to lose fat.

The Example Menus have been made to 1500kcal, 2000kcal, 2500kcal, 3000kcal and 3500kcal. If your Calorie value after your sums is 2225kcal and you are aiming to lose fat, you will choose the 2000kcal. If your Calorie value is 2189kcal and you are aiming to gain muscle you will pick the 2500kcal ration pack. The macros a little bit more "average" to ensure the Example Menus are applicable to everyone. For that reason I have used the mesomorph macros percentages, which is what I used to use for all my clients before I started using the somatotype ideas anyway.

Therefore, protein will be 35%, fats 30% and carbs 35% for each of the menus.

| 1500 Calorie Menu | | |
|---|---|---|
| **Breakfast** | **Sainsbury's Scottish Porridge Oats** 50g | Calories 178, Fat 4g Carbs 30g, Protein 5.5g |
| | **Sainsbury Blueberries** 100g | Calories 45, Fat 0.5g Carbs 9.1g, Protein 0.9g |
| | **MaxiNutrition Promax** (various flavours) Per 42g serving | Calories 152, Fat 2.4g Carbs 2.5g, Protein 30.0g |
| **Mid-morning** | **FAGE Total 0% Yoghurt** 1/2 cup 113g | Calories 64, Fat 0g Carbs 4.5g, Protein 11.5g |
| **Lunch** | **Chicken Breast** 1/2 skin and bone removed | Calories 138, Fat 3.1g Carbs 0g, Protein 27.6g |
| | **Avocado** 1/2 medium 75g | Calories 123, Fat 10.5g Carbs 5.8g, Protein 1.4g |
| | **Mixed Bean Salad** 1/2 Sainsbury's Mixed Bean Salad 135g drained | Calories 62, Fat 0.35g Carbs 11.3g, Protein 3.4g |
| | **Baby spinach** 42g 1 cup | Calories 10, Fat 0g Carbs 1g, Protein 1.5g |
| **Mid-afternoon** | **Almonds** 11 kernels 14g | Calories 91, Fat 7.5g Carbs 2.8g, Protein 3.1g |
| **Post Workout** | **MaxiNutrition Promax** (various flavours) Per 42g serving | Calories 152, Fat 2.4g Carbs 2.5g, Protein 30.0g |
| | **Banana** 1 medium 117g | Calories 105, Fat 0.44g Carbs 27g, Protein 1.3g |
| **Dinner** | **Salmon** Sainsbury Scottish fillet x 1 | Calories 214, Fat 12.3g Carbs 0.2g, Protein 25.5g |
| | **Sweet potato** 1 medium 114g | Calories 106, Fat 0.22g Carbs 23.6g, Protein 2.3g |
| | **Cauliflower** 1/2cup 62g | Calories 17, Fat 0.33g Carbs 2.5g, Protein 1.1g |

| | | |
|---|---|---|
| **Tomato** 1 small 91g | | Calories 16, Fat 0.22g Carbs 3.5g, Protein 0.8g |
| **Broccoli** 78g 1/2 cup chopped cooked | | Calories 33, Fat 0.33g Carbs 5.6g, Protein 1.9g |

### TOTAL CALORIES - 1506

| Protein - 147.8g = 591kcal (39%) | Fat - 43g = 387kcal (26%) | Carbs - 132g = 528 (35%) |
|---|---|---|

*Yes fats are a little low (30% ideal) and protein little high (35% ideal) but both are workable for the goal in hand. For carbs, considering most people following this 1500kcal Ration Pack will be wanting to lose body fat, this isn't a problem.*

### 2000 Calorie Menu

| | | |
|---|---|---|
| **Breakfast** | **Sainsbury Scottish Porridge Oats**75g | Calories 267, Fat 6g Carbs 45g, Protein 8.25g |
| | **Sainsbury Blueberries**100g | Calories 45, Fat 0.55g Carbs 9.1g, Protein 0.9g |
| | **MaxiNutrition Promax**(various flavours) Per 42g serving | Calories 152, Fat 2.4g Carbs 2.5g, Protein 30.0g |
| **Mid-morning** | **FAGE Total 2% Yoghurt**1/2 cup 114g | Calories 84, Fat 2.25g Carbs 4.5g, Protein 11.5g |
| | **Almonds**11 kernels 14g | Calories 91, Fat 7.5g Carbs 2.8g, Protein 3.1g |
| **Lunch** | **Sainsbury's Extra Lean Steak Mince**100g | Calories 123, Fat 4.55g Carbs 0g, Protein 20.5g |
| | **Cottage Cheese 100g** | Calories 70, Fat 1.2g Carbs 3.9g, Protein 11g |
| | **Mixed Bean Salad**1/2 Sainsbury's Mixed Bean Salad 135g drained | Calories 62, Fat 0.35g Carbs 11.3g, Protein 3.4g |
| | **Baby spinach**42g 1 cup | Calories 10, Fat 0g Carbs 1g, Protein 1.5g |
| **Mid-afternoon** | **Chicken Breast**1/2 skin and bone removed, cut into strips | Calories 138, Fat 3.1g Carbs 0g, Protein 27.6g |
| | **Avocado**1/2 medium 75g (with...) | Calories 123, Fat 10.5g Carbs 5.8g, Protein 1.4g |
| | **Extra Virgin Olive Oil Bertolli** 1 table spoon (... to make guacamole) | Calories 122, Fat 13.5g Carbs 0g 0%, Protein 0g |
| **Post Workout** | **MaxiNutrition Promax**(various flavours) Per 42g serving | Calories 152, Fat 2.4g Carbs 2.5g, Protein 30.0g |
| | **Banana**1 medium 117g | Calories 117, Fat 0.44g Carbs 27g, Protein 1.3g |
| **Dinner** | **Salmon**Sainsbury Scottish fillet x 1 | Calories 214, Fat 12.3g Carbs 0.2g, Protein 25.5g |
| | **Sweet potato**1 medium 114g | Calories 106, Fat 0.22g Carbs 23.6g, Protein 2.3g |
| | **Cauliflower**1/2cup 62g | Calories 17, Fat 0.33g Carbs 2.5g, Protein 1.1g |
| | **Tomato**1 small 91g | Calories 19, Fat 0.22g Carbs 3.5g, Protein 0.8g |
| | **Broccoli**78g 1/2 cup chopped cooked | Calories 33, Fat 0.33g Carbs 5.6g, Protein 1.9g |
| **Pre-bed** | **Tesco Pink Lady**1 apple 133g | Calories 66, Fat 0.11g Carbs 15.7g, Protein 0.5g |

### TOTAL CALORIES - 2011

| Protein - 183g = 732kcal (36.3%) | Fat - 68g = 612kcal (30.4%) | Carbs - 167g = 668 (33.3%) |
|---|---|---|

*Fats (30% ideal) and protein (35% ideal) are pretty much perfect. Carbs are a little low, but to be honest the "average" chicken breast, average apple, average sweet potato etc. will make this 2% of 2004 (around 40 Calories) negligible anyway.*

### 2500 Calorie Menu

| | | |
|---|---|---|
| **Breakfast** | **Sainsbury Scottish Porridge Oats**75g | Calories 267, Fat 6g |

| | | |
|---|---|---|
| | | Carbs 45g, Protein 8.25g |
| | Sainsbury Blueberries100g | Calories 45, Fat 0.55g<br>Carbs 9.1g, Protein 0.9g |
| | Tesco Pink Lady1/2 apple chopped 66.5g | Calories 33, Fat 0.055g<br>Carbs 7.85g, Protein 0.25g |
| | MaxiNutrition Promax(various flavours) Per 42g serving | Calories 152, Fat 2.4g<br>Carbs 2.5g, Protein 30.0g |
| Mid-morning | Egg Poached 2 large | Calories 144, Fat 10g<br>Carbs 0.8g, Protein 12.6g |
| | Sweet potato 1 medium 114g | Calories 106, Fat 0.22g<br>Carbs 23.6g, Protein 2.3g |
| Lunch | Sainsbury's Extra Lean Steak Mince 100g | Calories 123, Fat 4.55g<br>Carbs 0g, Protein 20.5g |
| | Cottage Cheese 100g | Calories 70, Fat 1.2g<br>Carbs 3.9g, Protein 11g |
| | Mixed Bean Salad 1/2 Sainsbury's Mixed Bean Salad 135g drained | Calories 62, Fat 0.35g<br>Carbs 11.3g, Protein 3.4g |
| | Baby spinach 63g 1.5 cups | Calories 13, Fat 0g<br>Carbs 1g, Protein 2.25g |
| | Almonds 11 kernels 14g | Calories 91, Fat 7.5g<br>Carbs 2.8g, Protein 3.1g |
| | Tesco Pink Lady 1/2 apple 66.5g | Calories 33, Fat 0.055g<br>Carbs 7.85g, Protein 0.25g |
| Mid-afternoon | Chicken Breast 100g, cut into strips | Calories 157, Fat 3.6g<br>Carbs 0g 0%, Protein 31g |
| | Avocado 1/2 medium 75g (with…) | Calories 123, Fat 10.5g<br>Carbs 5.8g, Protein 1.4g |
| | Extra Virgin Olive Oil Bertolli 1 table spoon (… to make guacamole) | Calories 122, Fat 13.5g<br>Carbs 0g 0%, Protein 0g |
| | Cashews 10kernels 14g | Calories 87, Fat 6.5g<br>Carbs 4.5g, Protein 2.5g |
| Post Workout | MaxiNutrition Promax (various flavours) Per 42g serving | Calories 152, Fat 2.4g<br>Carbs 2.5g, Protein 30.0g |
| | Banana 1 medium 117g | Calories 117, Fat 0.44g<br>Carbs 27g, Protein 1.3g |
| Dinner | Salmon Sainsbury's Scottish fillet x 1 | Calories 214, Fat 12.3g<br>Carbs 0.2g, Protein 25.5g |
| | Tilda Basmati Rice Cooked 100g | Calories 198, Fat 1.55g<br>Carbs 41g, Protein 5g |
| | Cauliflower 1/2cup 62g | Calories 17, Fat 0.33g<br>Carbs 2.5g, Protein 1.1g |
| | Tomato 1 small 91g | Calories 19, Fat 0.22g<br>Carbs 3.5g, Protein 0.8g |
| | Broccoli 78g 1/2 cup chopped cooked | Calories 33, Fat 0.33g<br>Carbs 5.6g, Protein 1.9g |
| | Orange 1 medium 160g | Calories 58, Fat 0g<br>Carbs 12.8g, Protein 1.6g |
| Pre-bed | Sainsbury's Blueberries 50g | Calories 23, Fat 0.27g<br>Carbs 4.6g, Protein 0.5g |
| | FAGE Total 0% Yoghurt 1/2 cup 113g | Calories 64, Fat 0g<br>Carbs 4.5g, Protein 11.5g |

| TOTAL CALORIES - 2523 | | |
|---|---|---|
| Protein - 209g = 836kcal (34%) | Fat - 85g = 765kcal (30%) | Carbs - 230g = 920kcal (36%) |

*Fats are bang on at 30%, carbs are a little high (ideal 35%) and protein a little low (ideal 35%). However, as we said for Ration Pack 2000kcal, the average of Calories within foods will more than make up for difference. The "average" chicken breast, egg, salmon and steak mince servings of a day could easily waiver by this much making this amount negligible and nothing to worry about.*

| 3000 Calorie Menu | | |
|---|---|---|
| Breakfast | Sainsbury Scottish Porridge Oats75g | Calories 267, Fat 6g<br>Carbs 45g, Protein 8.25g |
| | Sainsbury Blueberries100g | Calories 45, Fat 0.55g<br>Carbs 9.1g, Protein 0.9g |

| | | |
|---|---|---|
| | Tesco Pink Lady1/2 apple chopped 66.5g | Calories 33, Fat 0.055g Carbs 7.85g, Protein 0.25g |
| | MaxiNutrition Promax(various flavours) Per 42g serving | Calories 152, Fat 2.4g Carbs 2.5g, Protein 30.0g |
| Mid-morning | Egg Poached3 large | Calories 215, Fat 15g Carbs 1.2g, Protein 18.9g |
| | Sweet potato1 medium 114g | Calories 106, Fat 0.22g Carbs 23.6g, Protein 2.3g |
| Lunch | Sainsbury's Extra Lean Steak Mince100g | Calories 123, Fat 4.55g Carbs 0g, Protein 20.5g |
| | Cottage Cheese 150g | Calories 143, Fat 2.4g Carbs 7.87g, Protein 22.6g |
| | Mixed Bean Salad1/2 Sainsbury's Mixed Bean Salad 135g drained | Calories 62, Fat 0.35g Carbs 11.3g, Protein 3.4g |
| | Baby spinach63g 1.5 cups | Calories 13, Fat 0g Carbs 1g, Protein 2.25g |
| | Almonds11 kernels 14g | Calories 91, Fat 7.5g Carbs 2.8g, Protein 3.1g |
| | Tesco Pink Lady1/2 apple chopped 66.5g | Calories 33, Fat 0.055g Carbs 7.85g, Protein 0.25g |
| Mid-afternoon | Chicken Breast100g, cut into strips | Calories 157, Fat 3.6g Carbs 0g, Protein 31g |
| | Avocado1 medium 150g (with…) | Calories 247, Fat 21g Carbs 11.6g, Protein 2.8g |
| | Extra Virgin Olive Oil Bertolli1 table spoon (… to make guacamole) | Calories 121.5, Fat 13.5g Carbs 0g, Protein 0g |
| | Cashews10kernels 14g | Calories 86.5, Fat 6.5g Carbs 4.5g, Protein 2.5g |
| Post Workout | MaxiNutrition Promax(various flavours) Per 42g serving | Calories 152, Fat 2.4g Carbs 2.5g, Protein 30.0g |
| | Banana1 large 136g | Calories 135, Fat 0.55g Carbs 31g, Protein 1.5g |
| Dinner | SalmonSainsbury Scottish fillet x 1.5 | Calories 320, Fat 18.45g Carbs 0.2g, Protein 38.25g |
| | Tilda Basmati RiceCooked 100g | Calories 198, Fat 1.55g Carbs 41g, Protein 5g |
| | Cauliflower1cup 124g | Calories 35, Fat 0.66g Carbs 5g, Protein 2.2g |
| | Tomato2 small 182g | Calories 38, Fat 0.44g Carbs 7g, Protein 1.6g |
| | Broccoli156g 1 cup chopped cooked | Calories 66, Fat 0.66g Carbs 11.2g, Protein 3.8g |
| | Orange1 medium 160g | Calories 58, Fat 0g Carbs 12.8g, Protein 1.6g |
| Pre-bed | Sainsbury Blueberries100g | Calories 41, Fat 0.55g Carbs 9.1g, Protein 0.9g |
| | FAGE Total 0% Yoghurt3/4 cup 170g | Calories 96, Fat 0g Carbs 6.75g, Protein 17.25g |

| TOTAL CALORIES - 3034 | | |
|---|---|---|
| Protein - 251g = 1004kcal (33%) | Fat - 109g = 981kcal (32.5%) | Carbs - 262g = 1048 (34.5%) |

*Carbs (ideal 35%) are pretty much perfect. Fats (ideal 30%) are a little high, but it negligible as shown with other ration pack. The same can be said of Protein which is ever so slightly down (ideal 35%) but again, as we've shown in light of the average size and values of foods, it is fine.*

| 3500 Calorie Menu | | |
|---|---|---|
| Breakfast | Sainsbury Scottish Porridge Oats100g | Calories 356, Fat 8g Carbs 60g, Protein 11g |
| | Sainsbury Blueberries100g | Calories 45, Fat 0.55g, Carbs 9.1g, Protein 0.9g |
| | Tesco Pink Lady1/2 apple chopped 66.5g | Calories 33, Fat 0.055g Carbs 7.85g, Protein 0.25g |
| | MaxiNutrition Promax(various flavours) Per 42g serving | Calories 152, Fat 2.4g Carbs 2.5g, Protein 30.0g |

| | | |
|---|---|---|
| **Mid-morning** | **Egg Poached**3 large | Calories 215, Fat 15g Carbs 1.2g, Protein 18.9g |
| | **Sweet potato**1 large 130g | Calories 119, Fat 0.33g Carbs 26g, Protein 3g |
| **Lunch** | **Sainsbury's Extra Lean Steak Mince**125g | Calories 229, Fat 8.4g Carbs 0g, Protein 38.4g |
| | **Cottage Cheese 150g** | Calories 143, Fat 2.4g Carbs 7.8g, Protein 22.6g |
| | **Mixed Bean Salad**1 x Sainsbury's Mixed Bean Salad 270g drained | Calories 124, Fat 0.7g Carbs 22.6g, Protein 6.8g |
| | **Baby spinach**63g 1.5 cups | Calories 13, Fat 0 Carbs 1g, Protein 2.25g |
| | **Almonds**11 kernels 14g | Calories 91, Fat 7.5g Carbs 2.8g, Protein 3.1g |
| | **Tesco Pink Lady**1/2 apple chopped 66.5g | Calories 33, Fat 0.055g Carbs 7.85g, Protein 0.25g |
| **Mid-afternoon** | **Chicken Breast**125g, cut into strips | Calories 197, Fat 4.5g Carbs 0g, Protein 39g |
| | **Avocado**1 medium 150g (with…) | Calories 247, Fat 21g Carbs 11.6g, Protein 2.8g |
| | **Extra Virgin Olive Oil Bertolli**1 table spoon (… to make guacamole) | Calories 122, Fat 13.5g Carbs 0g, Protein 0g |
| | **Cashews**10kernels 14g | Calories 86.5, Fat 6.5g Carbs 4.5g, Protein 2.5g |
| **Post Workout** | **MaxiNutrition Promax**(various flavours) Per 42g serving | Calories 152, Fat 2.4g Carbs 2.5g, Protein 30.0g |
| | **Banana**2 large 272g | Calories 270, Fat 1.1g Carbs 62g, Protein 3g |
| **Dinner** | **Salmon**Sainsbury Scottish fillet x 1.5 | Calories 320, Fat 18.45g Carbs 0.2g, Protein 38.25g |
| | **Tilda Basmati Rice**Cooked 100g | Calories 198, Fat 1.55g Carbs 41g, Protein 5g |
| | **Cauliflower**1cup 124g | Calories 35, Fat 0.66g Carbs 5g, Protein 2.2g |
| | **Tomato**2 small 182g | Calories 38, Fat 0.44g Carbs 7g, Protein 1.6g |
| | **Broccoli**156g 1 cup chopped cooked | Calories 66, Fat 0.66g Carbs 11.2g, Protein 3.8g |
| | **Orange**1 medium 160g | Calories 58, Fat 0g Carbs 12.8g, Protein 1.6g |
| **Pre-bed** | **Sainsbury Blueberries**100g | Calories 45, Fat 0.55g Carbs 9.1g, Protein 0.9g |
| | **FAGE Total 0% Yoghurt**3/4 cup 169.5g | Calories 96, Fat 0g Carbs 6.75g, Protein 17.25g |

| TOTAL CALORIES - 3484 | | |
|---|---|---|
| Protein - 286g = 1144kcal (33%) | Fat - 117g = 1053kcal (30%) | Carbs - 322g = 1288 (37%) |

To reiterate, I appreciate that these Example Menus would mean you eat the same food day in day out and are also not being 100% specific to your Calorie requirements. As I said at the start, for soldiers living off Ration Packs that is the reality. It's not ideal, but it's ok for a period of time. It serves a purpose: ease and fuel. The idea behind these Menus is no different. The ease should be that you could go to the supermarket on a weekend and in one shop buy a (relatively) short list of things that you can then prepare and ensure you have in your Example Menu sorted. The Calories may not be 100% accurate, but as long as you are below your needs from the equations if your goal is to lose body fat and above your needs from the equations if your goal is to gain muscle, the science will work.

I appreciate that some of you will be looking at the Example Menus and thinking, "I can't do this, I don't like salmon". Or "I don't eat red meat". Or "I don't like eggs". Or

"I can't stand the idea of THIS with THAT" (don't knock it until you've tried it is all I can say. Like sweet potato with eggs; sweet potato goes with pretty much everything - try it with Total Yoghurt!).

What I've done is put together a list (it's not extensive, but it gives you ideas) of alternate foods you can use to switch in for those you don't like or find too repetitive. Just try to switch like for like, not only protein for protein, carb for carb and fat for fat, but if it's a fatty protein, like salmon, you need to switch this for a similar fatty fish like mackerel. You need those good fish oils and omega 3s.

If you are switching the Total Yoghurt out, remember is has protein, fats and carbs, so if you are switching out because you don't eat dairy, look for a good alternative that has similar macros. If you just switch in coconut yoghurt (which is great) the likelihood is that the fat content will be WAY higher and protein lower, so you may have to look at cutting out the olive oil elsewhere or having less avocado to allow for the excess fat from coconut oil. You don't want to switch one thing in and see your 2000kcal go to 2150kcal with one simple addition.

## Alternates

| PROTEIN | |
| --- | --- |
| Chicken breast | Tuna |
| Chicken thighs (with skin on 1 or 2 times per week) | Mackerel |
| Turkey breast | Sardines |
| Turkey mince | Trout |
| Lean mince beef | Haddock |
| Steak | Cod |
| Lean Gammon | Pollock |
| Lean Ham | Prawns |
| Lean pork | Crab |

| DAIRY | |
| --- | --- |
| Total Greek Yoghurt 2% | Other Greek yoghurts are often higher in sugar and lower in protein. I recommend always going for Total. Whether 0%, 2% or normal depends onCalorieand fat needs. |
| Cheese | Cottage cheese is best as it's more high protein and lower fat than most other cheese sources. If you do choose other cheeses, aim for as high protein as possible. Fat content depends on your calorie needs. |
| Whole Milk | Better than skimmed or semi-skimmed as more nutritious. |
| Quark | Similar to Total yoghurt. Almost a halfway between cottage cheese and yoghurt. Can be very high protein and low carb. So a good substitute for either. |

| PROTEIN SUPPLEMENTS | |
|---|---|
| Whey protein isolate | Whey protein concentrate |
| Casein protein | Egg protein |
| Beef Protein | |

| VEGETARIAN PROTEIN SUPPLEMENTS | |
|---|---|
| Whey protein isolate | Whey protein concentrate |
| Casein protein | |

| CARBOHYDRATE | |
|---|---|
| Potatoes- boiled or baked ideally | Rice cakes |
| Quinoa | Popcorn (no salted/caramelised) |
| Wild rice | Bulgurwheat |
| Basmati rice | Wholemeal, stoneground bread |
| Rye crisp bread | |

| VEGETABLES | |
|---|---|
| Bok Choi | Brussel Sprouts |
| Spinach | Aubergine |
| Kale | Courgette |
| Green beans | Squashes |
| Asparagus | Mixedstir-fry |
| Peas | Mixed green salad |

| FRUIT | |
|---|---|
| Strawberries | Peach |
| Raspberries | Pear |
| Blackberries | Kiwi fruit |
| Cherries | Pineapple |
| Grapes | Mango |
| Nectarine | |

*Remember, fruit is nutrient dense (packed full of vitamins and minerals) but also Calorie dense. If exchanging half an apple for something else, it may not be equivalent in Calories to just eat half a mango. Check Calories where possible.*

| FATS |
|---|

| Avocado | Olive oil |
| --- | --- |
| Coconut oil | Nuts and 100% nut butters<br>(No palm or hydrogenated oils) |
| Olives | Fish<br>(oily fish like salmon, mackerel, trout, sardines especially) |

Like the Example Menus themselves, these lists are quite simple and perhaps not as restrictive as you may imagine a "diet" should be. I think you'll agree the whole Example Menu idea is kind of middle of the road. It's not so restrictive that people don't conform, yet not too inclusive that people go crazy and overeat. The point yet again is that everyone is different. For example, I can take more calories than Rachel McAdams, yet it's fair to say Chris Hemsworth (all 6 feet 3 of him) can take more calories than me. We all need to be aware of our needs.

The Example Menus give you guidelines if you are still struggling with the difference between carbs, fats and protein sources. We don't want you getting 70-80% of your Calories from fruit because it seems healthy and is easy to pick up and eat with no preparation needed. We need you to put the time into preparing your food. Like anything, the more you work with it, the more you understand it. We need you to start to understand your macros, hit your protein needs, get some good fats in and make up the rest of your Calories with sensible carbohydrate choices like those listed in the carbohydrate choices list.

The Example Menus and the alternate lists above just show examples of the way you should try to structure your meals. They aren't for everyone. If the idea of them doesn't work for you, that's fine. Choose another option laid out in this book. If you do like the Example Menus idea, eating this way (like the 8 Simple Rules and 20 Foods to Eat) should help you keep your meals and days organised and regular. Thus stopping you from reaching for the biscuits, sweets or chocolate as you shouldn't be getting any afternoon sugar crashes at work! Equally, eating this way should ensure you have enough energy for your training and eat regularly enough that you won't be breaking down any muscle tissue through lack of supplying the body with what it needs.

# Chapter 8: Supplements

Supplements are a contentious issue when it comes to nutrition. There are some who swear by them and others who chastise them. If I'm honest, I can see both sides. In my opinion supplements have got a bad name largely because of the way supplements companies push them and advertise them.

Most supplement companies don't just concentrate on the protein and vitamin supplements (which I believe are worthwhile at least having on hand to take when needed), but push fat burners and other less moral supplements as well.

## Fat burners - the Con Artists of the Fitness Industry

In my opinion, fat burners are largely a con. Any company that has a specific fat burner, let alone started out as a fat burner (i.e. their first product was a fat burner) is focusing on the industry in completely the wrong way and is partly to blame for peoples' backward approach to fitness. Being healthy and fit may be at the very basic level about looking good, but following the guidelines in this book will hopefully help you achieve the body you want while also helping you to become healthier and fitter in the process. I would always suggest focussing on health and fitness, as aesthetics will come if you do that.

Simply taking a fat burner does not do this. There is no education. No nutrition and in many cases no effort! It's telling people that they can take a short cut. Avoid training and eating sensibly and instead take a pill. It is also taking advantage of peoples insecurities to make money. My advice: don't pay through the nose for what (in the UK anyway) is probably just green tea extract, chilli powder, orange peel, caffeine and anything else that may have been shown to raise the metabolism at some point.

## Multivitamins

In terms of more conventional supplements, if you are eating following the 8 Simple Rules and the 20 Foods to Eat, you are probably getting all the essential vitamins and minerals you need in your diet as well as adequate fat to absorb the fat soluble vitamins and to perform the various roles fatty acids do in the body. However, the food we get in supermarkets, whether fruits and vegetables or meats and fish are not quite what they once were.

Intensive farming and how the plants and animals are fed mean the quality and content (in terms of vitamins, minerals, phytochemicals and even macros) is not always as good as it should be or once was. Therefore, taking a high quality multivitamin can be a good idea. It can cover the bases that may be missing from even a healthy diet in today's world.

Furthermore, if you find yourself unable to eat "well" for a few days due to holiday, travel, stag do, wedding; whatever it may be. A multivitamin can be a great addition just to stave off illness and/or injury. I see no reason why topping up with a multivit in these times should be seen as a negative.

## Vitamin C

Again, even if you choose not to take the multivitamin every day, it's worth having one in the cupboard for if you go away and can't eat as much veg or as healthily as you normally like. Moreover, if you become unwell, a multivitamin might help you get over whatever it is. especially if you are struggling to eat. In a similar vein, I sometimes think a vitamin C tablet is worth having on standby. If you become unwell or have to go away with work, or even on holiday, and find yourself eating a little less broccoli and oranges, take a vitamin C tablet. Check your multivitamin for its percentage of vitamin C RDA. It may be pretty low unless it's a very expensive one. In that case get a separate Vit C for these low times.

## Vitamin D

The only two supplements I would suggest you do take daily are vitamin D and Omega 3. Vitamin D is something a surprisingly high number of us are deficient in. As you've probably heard, Vitamin D isn't really a vitamin as it isn't attained from our food. Natural sunlight allows the body to create vitamin D. It's estimated that up to 80% of the population could be vitamin D deficient! Especially when you consider our ability to manufacture it gets worse with age and the higher our body fat percentage. Also, people with darker skin living in the UK will have more problems as their skin pigmentation screens out the relatively limited sunlight we get more effectively.

All in all, I recommend a vitamin D supplement to prevent the side effect of dietary calcium not being absorbed. Vit D is essential to do this. Calcium in turn is essential for brain cell signalling as well as bone and tooth development/formation. Low vitamin D levels are also associated with increased loss of muscle strength/mass as we age, increased risk of cancers, lower levels of immunity, higher blood pressure, development of neurological disorders and development of diabetes. Need I say more? I sincerely recommend a Vitamin D supplement.

## Omega 3

The second supplement I wholeheartedly believe we should all be taking is Omega 3. The Omega 3s are EPA and DHA (found in fish oils and algae) and ALA (found in flax and walnuts). EPA and DHA originate in algae, which fish eat and thus concentrated high amounts of these beneficial fats can be derived from them. Now you could argue that if you eat enough oily fish (salmon, mackerel, sardines etc) that contain these omega 3s, then a supplement isn't needed. I do agree to a point. The problem is, like the points above about the quality of fruits and veg we eat, is that many of the fish we eat today are farmed and thus do we really get the natural goodness we would've done from wild fish?

Omega-3s are very important for many health reasons including cardiovascular function, nervous system function, brain development and immune health. Still not convinced? Well, with the close relationship to brain and nervous tissue, research has shown that low DHA consumption is associated with memory loss, difficulty concentrating and even Alzheimer's disease. Alzheimer's is a horrible disease and one which I personally wouldn't want to see anyone I care about go through. Hence I recommend anyone close to me to supplement with Omega 3 capsules. Especially those who don't/won't eat oily fish.

Omega 3s also help keep cell membranes (all our cells have a lipid bilayer) fluid and permeable. By eating fish oils we ensure they stay that way. Ingesting too many saturated fats (which are solid at room temperature) with a lack of ingesting enough omega 3s leads to more rigid cell membranes and then a lack of permeability: i.e. things can't enter the cell properly. This can literally affect the whole body. Our cells also require these good omega fats for repair and regeneration.

If you're still to be convinced, how about the fact that omega-3s help muscle cells become more sensitive to insulin and help white fat cells decrease; meaning more nutrients to muscle tissue than fat, helping with your health and aesthetics.

Couldn't we all just ensure we eat organic oily fish instead of taking a processed supplement? Well, yes. But the problem is that our omega 3: omega 6 balance should ideally be 1:1. In the western world, it's more like 1:20 for a vast majority and 1:4 for those of us that don't overeat processed foods, vegetable oils and animals fed on corn or soy and who actually eat oily fish. Decades ago this wasn't a problem as we ate mainly wild animals, but not so with today's intensive farming. Even countries that eat insects fare better than the UK/US where we don't, as insects have a good amount of omega 3s.

The answer then is to try and ingest 1-3grams of omega 3s a day and the best way to do this is via oily fish and to top up with an omega 3 supplement. Not cod liver oil, but DHA and EPA. Avoid trans fats (obviously) as these interfere with the body's processing of omega 3s. Avoid vegetable oils and other omega 6 products as much as possible (you'll get enough anyway!), so don't buy an omega 3, 6, 9 supplement. There will be little omega 3 and way too much 6, thus not helping with the imbalance at all. If you still don't want to take an omega 3 supplement daily, then consider taking it on days when you don't eat any oily fish. That way at least you are getting something every day.

## ZMA

A final supplement that I take myself and advise to those who either want to build muscle and are over 30, or have a problem sleeping (either because they are carb cycling - known to cause sleep problems in some or just a stressed person who sleeps badly) is ZMA. ZMA is Zinc, Magnesium and Vitamin B6. Overall, ZMA is a recovery aid and is mostly used by athletes and bodybuilders. Studies with ZMA and a placebo group showed that those taking ZMA had testosterone and strength increases compared to the placebo. As magnesium is also associated with sleep, the idea is that sleep and recovery is also heightened.

If taking ZMA isn't your thing, but you have issues sleeping, then you can also get a magnesium spray that you spray on the back of the elbows or knees. Warning: it does cause an itch at first! This is supposedly illustrating a deficiency, but as you repeat the use, this lessens. I have tried the spray and did find I slept better. You should be able to get the zinc, magnesium and B6 you need when ingesting a good quality diet, especially if following the 8 Simple Rules and 20 Foods to Eat. However if you are following a more IIFYM style diet or just want to make sure at times when your diet may be off track, ZMA can be a good one to have in the cupboard.

## Creatine

Creatine is one of the few supplements that has time and time again been shown to make a real difference in studies and has also been shown to be safe without any side effects. This is largely due to the fact that it is produced naturally by the body in the kidneys, liver and pancreas at a rate of about 1-2 grams/day. It can also be obtained from food, particularly red meat. Around 90-95% of creatine in the body is found in muscle.

In terms of what it does, creatine is involved in one of 3 energy systems that allows us to take part in sport and training or simply move and live life. It is involved in energy production for short bursts of high intensity exercise like sprints or lifting weights; and hence its popularity with body builders and those training with resistance.

My advice would be that if you are training to lose weight, you could take creatine as it will help you train a little longer when working really hard and it could help you produce a little more muscle short term. However, it is not essential by any means. For those training to gain muscle, creatine has been shown again and again to be very beneficial when working towards this goal. I would therefore say it's worth considering.

If you do decide to use creatine (I have on and off a number of times) consume 3-5 grams of creatine per day. This can either be taken with water, in a shake of some sort or can even be dissolved in a warm but not boiling drink like green tea. It can be taken before and/or after workout sessions in your pre/post workout shakes, although studies have shown uptake is better post workout due to utilisation during training. Most manufacturers recommend cycling on and off, although no side effects have been shown from supplementing indefinitely. I would agree that taking a break every 12-16weeks is worthwhile. Just like you would with your training.

## Beta-Alanine

I don't want to go down the route of including every supplement a brand would sell. However, beta alanine is one I do take myself from time to time. It's a supplement which has been shown to increase endurance, great for anyone wanting to train hard for sports performance, weightloss or muscle gain. Beta-alanine is an amino acid that combines with histidine in the body to form a dipeptide called Carnosine. Peptides are strings of amino-acids, which are precursors to full proteins. It's thought that muscles with higher levels of this dipeptide Carnosine can contract for longer and with more force. Therefore beta-alanine is thought to lead to increases in strength, endurance and as a result, muscle gain and fatloss.

As stated above, creatine has been shown time and time again to aid muscle growth and fatloss, well combining creatine and beta-alanine is thought to lead to more muscle gain and more body fat lost than just creatine alone. I'm not one for pushing any supplement. you don't *need* to take anything, but it's better to explain here than wish I had later.
Lastly, people tend to experience "tingles" from beta-alanine supplementation, due to its effect on capillaries. An itching or tingling around the lips, hairline or ears is commonplace and nothing to worry about. As your body get used to the supplement this tends to subside unless you keep upping the amount you take, which isn't necessary for the endurance, muscle gain and fatloss benefits.


## Protein

The supplement of supplements. The old faithful and the subject of so many discussions. My experience with protein supplements and trainees/trainers alike is something that really tickles me. It seems people are either completely obsessed with protein supplementation and carry it around with them everywhere, drink it within seconds of finishing their training, panic if they forget their shake and generally feel like protein supplementation is THE number one facet to get right when training for fat loss or muscle gain.

Conversely, you find those people that (in my opinion) find it cool and contrary to tell everyone who will listen that they don't take any supplements and can get everything they need from food. Often they believe supplements are a complete waste of money and chastise anyone who take them. On one hand, I understand their point as many supplement companies are over charging and many (as mentioned above with fat burners) are immoral; using obvious steroid users to advertise their products while supporting the lies these people make around their "natural" physiques to sell products. To chastise supplements altogether because a few ruin it for the masses is a mistake; protein or otherwise.

It's true that you don't NEED supplements and that you could get everything you need from food. That's a fact. However, you could also get to and from work every day by walking, even if it would take an hour and a half to do so. You don't do that though, not unless you have or want to. You take the bus, or drive, or train, or cycle. Why? It's faster, more convenient and should save you time, so is usually preferable even if it costs a little more. I don't need to spell it out from there do I? Supplements are the train ride to work. You don't need it. You can do without it, but it can make life more convenient and easier and get you to your end point a little faster.

If someone is training before work, at lunch or after work and they wouldn't be able to eat within 30minutes of training, there are reasons to take a protein shake with them and drink it following training. There is a supposed "window of opportunity" within the first hour or so after training (more likely 30minutes) where the body is primed for taking on carbs and protein to refuel and repair. If you are someone who would go to the gym, then get caught up with work and life for 2hrs before eating, you could be wasting some of your efforts in the gym; whether trying to lose fat or gain muscle.

A protein and carbohydrate meal in the form of a protein shake and a banana is a perfect way to end a session. In fact, if you are taking in 30g of protein, you ideally should be taking in 60g of carbs. If this isn't in the form of fruit, then dextrose/maltodextrin is equally as good, even though it is less nutritious in terms of vitamins and minerals. I would always opt for fruit at that point if possible.

## Unnatural

There's been a big shift in recent years about training naturally and eating 'cleanly". This is superb and should certainly be the way the human race should go. Avoiding processed foods and hopefully solving some serious lifestyle diseases in the process. However, supplements aren't "unnatural" as such. Yes, they are processed. I agree with that, but whey or casein protein supplements are simply milk (which was the old school bodybuilder of the 1970s post workout shake) with the fat and carbs removed. Whey and casein are the two constituent proteins of milk. You've had them many, many times, whether in tea or coffee, on cereal. You don't drink milk? Well, I hate to break it to you, but you've still had them (wait for it) from your mother's breast. Yes, as I said on page 21, breast milk is also made up of whey and contains casein too.

My advice therefore is simple. Protein supplementation is neither to be avoided and chastised or loved and devoted. It isn't completely necessary and if you miss it once or twice, so be it. Don't lose any sleep. Equally, it isn't the horror of the fitness industry that some people make out, though the way it is advertised by some companies, I can see why this would seem the case. If you do want to loathe a supplement, leave that for fat burners!

Protein supplementation definitely has its place, whether to help with recovery post workout, to bridge the gap before proper food can be prepared and eaten, or (as in the Example Menus above) to turn a high carb meal like porridge into a high protein meal by stirring in some protein powder. This also makes it a nice flavour like vanilla or strawberry which if you ask me is a far better way to start the day that either skipping breakfast or just having carbs in the form of jam and toast or porridge with honey. Yes, eggs on toast would be the ideal, but it takes a little longer and what if you are out of eggs? Protein porridge takes 3minutes: 2 to microwave the porridge, 20 seconds to stir in the protein powder and 40seconds to eat it. Ok, for a Marine maybe! But you get my point.

If you are still hell bent on never letting a single penny of your hard earned cash go to the many, many companies producing protein supplements, fair enough. I do understand your sentiments. However, I'd advise that along with the multivitamins and omega 3s, you have some protein powder in the cupboard at home just in case. Choose a flavour you'll like (vanilla, chocolate, peanut butter etc.) and use it if you have a low protein day before going to bed or on a day you may struggle to eat well at work, pack it just in case. I would advise having it post workout, but if you don't want to, grab a small whole milk and a banana or even some Total Yoghurt and a banana.

For those that are vegan or vegetarian and probably tearing your hair out at all the dairy I'm advising, fear not. I have recently convinced the protein supplement brand I work with and have done for over 6years to produce a vegan protein. For anyone wanting to follow a plant based diet try pea, hemp, brown rice, potato or even soy proteins. Do be aware that they can taste a little earthy at times, but that's just a price you pay for your choices. Again, I am vegetarian, so I totally respect the choice. Like anyone else, I recommend vegans/vegetarians have a protein product in the cupboard and use it at least post workout. Many plant based eaters struggle to get in enough protein, a pea or soy protein powder can be a real godsend when trying to lose body fat or gain muscle on a plant based diet. Don't shy away from it; give it a go!

# Chapter 9: Conclusion

There it is. Nine chapters of nutritional knowledge downloaded into one (not so) short ebook. As I said from the start, the idea was not to teach the science and confuse you. This is not a text for PTs or people wanting to get into nutrition. This is aimed at someone wanting to lose fat, gain muscle, perform well at life or sport, or someone just wanting to be healthier. It is written to give you three methods of achieving a healthier and fitter lifestyle or obtain a figure/physique that you will be happy/proud of. Hopefully either or both will be achievable for anyone reading this book and implementing its content will help with other facets of your life.

Where I think other books I have read fall down, is that they try to provide a "one size fits all for fat loss/body composition" because that is what people want. Gyms and magazine and even supplement companies sell us the idea that in four weeks you can look like A or B, when in reality that's not true. At least not for 90% of us. Everyone is different, not just our starting point, but our genetics, our timetables and our will power. Therefore, not only does there have to be some work from you to get to the end goal, but your starting point will determine how long it takes to get to your end point. You need to workout your Calorie needs, your protein, fat and carb needs, or you have to stick to 8 Simple Rules combined with trying to eat 20 Foods to Eat as often as possible. You do that for as long as it takes. in my mind, its a lifestyle choice and you should do it forever, mixing in with the expected naughty days when socialising or celebrating.

I've tried to be honest and upfront. Tell it how it is and give you ways to make it work for you. But if this all sounds like too much hassle, then ask yourself if this is really that important to you? If it's not, that's fine. Life, family or cake is more important. That's your choice, for your life. Just don't look for the quick fixes, they are usually expensive, either financially or health wise. There are no quick fixes or easy routes. If doing things properly isn't for you, then don't do them.


Remember this:

1.      *If it was easy, everyone would have it.*
1.      *Anything worth having is hard to get.*


## Moving forward

Try things, test them, assess, adjust, test, re-adjust etc. Find what works for you, your lifestyle, your body, your work, your willpower. Just don't give up. If you don't, I (almost) guarantee that the ideas in this book, coupled with an intense, progressive training programme, will give you everything you need to be looking "the part" on your next holiday in your shorts or bikini while also being fit and healthy on the inside to go with it.

## 10 things to take away if nothing else:

1.      **Remember the 8 Simple Rules**. Only eat high quality food choices. Real, natural, foods instead of refined foods. If it hasn't grown from the ground or in a tree, lived, swam, ran etc. Don't eat it except on your Metabolic Meal day from time to time. Get some sleep! 8-8.5hrs each day on average will help with your goal.

1.      **Calories in and Calories out trumps everything else**. If you pay no attention to Calories then you could be overeating and you will not get the results you want if that is the case. You may get fitter, but you won't necessarily be making the progress you want, to be able see the figure or physique you want to see in the mirror. To lose body fat, ensure you are in a Calorie deficit (10-20%, no more!). To gain muscle, ensure you are in a Calorie surplus. Use the formulas in the book to do this. I've included them because they work!

1.      **Ensure you eat enough protein to maintain the lean muscle mass you have**. Too many people, especially those eating a plant based diet, don't get enough protein. Whether you follow the 8 Simple Rules and eat a palm or 1-1.5 palm size servings of protein with each meal, or follow the somatotype percentages to work out your needs and spread through the day. Don't skimp on protein. It will help you burn body fat and build muscle. Both will help you achieve health, fitness and aesthetics.

1.      **Don't avoid fat**. Your somatotype will determine your percentage needs, or just follow the 8 Simple Rules and have a thumb/golfball amount of fats with your meals. However you do it, ensure high quality "good fats" from oily fish, avocado, meat, olive oil, butter and nuts. Without these you will be hampering your fat loss and your body's ability to work optimally. Avoid trans fats and vegetable oils, and consider an omega 3 supplement especially if you don't eat oily fish.

1.      **Don't fear carbs**. Again! Don't fear carbs! You need carbs, just aim to get them from real foods like vegetables, potatoes, sweet potatoes, basmati rice, oats, berries and fruits. Avoid processed versions as much as possible. Vegetables wise, eat 1-2 servings with every meal. If you work with the 20 Foods to Eat and 8 Simple Rules this will become habit and that change alone will help you leaps and bounds in terms of health, fitness and aesthetics.

1.      **Eat the number of meals a day that suits your lifestyle/working day but ensure a good distribution of the food and macronutrients that allows you to most consistently stick with this new way of eating**. To maximise your training, I would advise trying to eat 20g of protein every 3hrs if this works for you. If not, then don't. Remember, Calories are most important overall!

1.      However you are choosing to monitor your food intake and follow my plan, **have a "Metabolic Meal" once a week or twice a month** to ensure you can keep to this long-term. If choosing to Calorie/carb cycle, this will be your high meal. Remember, once you've finished that meal and have left the table, that's it. Back to good eating for the week. Try to stick to "good" foods for at least some of your Metabolic Meal/high Cal/carb day. It's not just an excuse to binge!

1.      **Drink lots of water**. Water not only helps you feel full, it is necessary for all bodily functions, including fat metabolism. Drink between 750ml-1litre per 20kg of bodyweight. For a 60kg women that's 3litres. For every hour of exercise, add another 1litre. A good piece of advice is "drink like it's your job". Try it, this along

with eating veg with every meal will make huge changes in your health, fitness and aesthetics alone.

1.      **Supplement as you feel comfortable**. I would advise a multivitamin, vitamin D and some omega 3 fish oil daily as these tend to be areas we all suffer from deficiencies in. I also advise taking a protein supplement post training and to enable some meals (like breakfast) that are notoriously rushed, skipped or carb only, to be a protein based meal.

1.      **Limit coffee and alcohol**. One cup of coffee a day can be good as it raises metabolism, but any more can have negative effects on absorption of key micronutrients which can hamper fat loss, not to mention sleep which aids recovery and fat loss. One alcoholic drink a day at the very most. Where possible, try to limit to a couple at the weekend but DON'T binge. Don't forget to factor alcohol into your MyFitnessPal Calorie totals if you are using a Calorie counting strategy. Remember, alcohol is a poison and it will hamper fat loss/muscle synthesis. However, if you want it, have it, enjoy it then adhere to your plan.

## Final point

Being aesthetic is very important to people these days, but it will only get you so far. Yes, it may help you be more confident or even find a partner, but the deep lying issues as to why it is so important to you will always be there. My experience is that even when you've achieved the goal you've set out to achieve, you are unlikely to leave it there. Chasing the perfect figure or physique isn't always healthy and I've seen it lead to eating disorders, the use of drugs like steroids and even plastic surgery. Don't fall into that trap.

Use the HEALTHY eating guidelines in this book to make your journey is more about health and fitness. Aesthetics will come in part off the back of this, but it won't be ALL about aesthetics, which is far healthier in the long run. Your body is THE most important and precious thing you will ever own. Do not misuse it. Don't take it for granted. Save spending your money on clothes, alcohol and frivolous things and instead spend some money on good quality food and amazing experiences with people you care about. Your body will thank you and will last a lot longer.
That's it. Eat well, train hard and reap the rewards. Above all, #BeMoreCommando and never give up.

# Chapter 10: Case Studies

It's easy for me to write this book and expect you just to take my word for everything I've said. From your point of view, there are thousands of books out there on this subject. Not to mention the millions of trainers and nutritionists selling plans and programmes. Why this book then? I hope the information given across these ten chapters has been honest, well presented, easy to follow and inspiring. If it has, great. I'm pleased. If not, then the following may help.

In an attempt to inspire you to give one of the nutritional plan options in this book a go, especially if you are still unconvinced that you can change your health and fitness and therefore your figure/physique, I have written a short paragraph on six different people I have helped to make significant changes to their life. Some a little, some a lot. Some have obtained the cover model style physique they wanted, others have realised that there's more to life for them than that. However, all achieved what I think is the nirvana when starting this nutrition and fitness journey. Health. They all became healthier and their lives better because of it, both short term and hopefully long term. In turn, I hope there's at least one of these case studies that resonates with you and will inspire you to follow suit.

## 1.Late Thirties Male - Gym Beginner

This individual had two major challenges. First, he had never really done any exercise other than playing football. He had never trained with weights, ever. We had to change this. Second, he also had ME/Chronic Fatigue Syndrome. At the time, this would hit him at least once a week and often meant a day or two off work when it did. Our aim was to add muscle and lower body fat. His visceral fat (the fat around his organs) was at the red (danger) level so we had to make him healthier first and hope aesthetics and fitness followed. We completely changed his diet. We weren't overly restrictive other than he had a Calorie target which he had to stick to. Other than that, the 8 Simple Rules and 20 Foods to Eat were the main aims of the food ingested. Over 10 weeks he lost 6kg of fat and gained 1kg of muscle (figures via BodyScan UK so very accurate). His visceral fat dropped from dangerous to just below average. Most significantly though, he only had one bout of CFS in the 10 weeks we worked together and since the 10 weeks, as he has kept training and kept eating well (due to completely seeing the benefits), he has almost completely removed CFS from his life.

## 2.Forties Professional Female - weight-loss and depression

This individual had a high pressure and prestigious job. This meant stress and busy hours. It also at one point meant some problems with depression. Quite often, she could only train once a week. Where she could, she aimed for twice. This meant we had to affect her fat loss, which was the primary goal, via nutrition in the main. Cutting straight to the point, we gave her a Calorie target and she used MyFitnessPal to log everything she ate. At first we were more restrictive than necessary with the 8 Simple Rules and 20 Foods to Eat, actually cutting out certain foods. This was partly to make things simpler but also to enable the odd "naughty" snack at work which was unfortunately a common occurrence. By using MyFitnessPal religiously, she not only lost a considerable amount of weight by removing the unhealthy processed foods and at times excess alcohol, she also put much of the depression in the past. This process was not given a timeline, but was simply to change the thought process of how food should be eaten and how exercise can be a de-stresser. She now uses hard interval training at least once and often three times a week to stay fit and keep stress at bay. An annual work health assessment put her VO2 max at the level of someone in their twenties.

### 3.Early Twenties Male - cover model dream

Despite using the gym regularly and playing football frequently this individual could not achieve any real changes in his physique. His aim was to produce a muscular yet lean physique. The Cristiano Ronaldo look. When he started he was far from this; just a normal 20 year old male. His job was not stressful and eating clean was not going to be an issue. He was prepared to cut out the nightlife which had previously been a BIG part of his life. Over 3 months he ate a small Calorie surplus, cut out the drinking and socialising to a couple of times a month and trained religiously (and intensely) 4-6 times a week. He gained a considerable amount of muscle in that time. He then spent 6 weeks on a slight Calorie deficit, ensuring he hit specific macros (as he did when in a surplus) and by utilising HIIT alongside his weight training leaned up to create a cover model physique. When hitting the beach that summer he was the envy of all his friends who he had kept his nutrition/training a secret from. He has carried on training and using Calorie calculations to ensure he holds onto his muscle and can lean up to reveal a six pack over a few weeks whenever he wants to, despite returning to a few more nights out these days.

### 4.Mid Thirties Male - lifestyle disease waiting to happen

After years of eating badly, drinking and doing no exercise this individual, almost out of the blue, decided to do something about it. Utilising a Calorie deficit, specific macros and MyFitnessPal to eat foods from the 8 Simple Rules and 20 Foods to Eat, he attacked a hard training programme over 3 months to really throw himself in the deep end. By sticking with it and seeing some great results he continued for another 9months, getting advice from different people, trainers and coaches, reading nutrition articles and posts online and generally trying to educate himself. Prior issues including skin problems have completely cleared up and his appearance is totally different. He now looks like a slim late twenties male, whereas at the start he looked like a very unhealthy and overweight mid to late thirties male. I would say this man has added decades to his life by making changes at the point he did and sticking with it. He is now so interested in the subject he has started the process of doing nutrition courses in a bid to inspire others.

### 5.Late Twenties Female - eating disorder

This individual was perhaps in as much danger as anyone I have worked with. She was years into an eating disorder, one which was completely controlling her life and decisions at times. I admit to not necessarily paying enough attention to the psychological aspects of the problem, which I now understand far more. My Marine background took over and we attacked the problem head on. By using the gym and hard training as a new focus for her obsessive nature and to help remove depression, while ensuring healthy food choices around the 8 Simple Rules and 20 Foods to Eat, she was able to change her figure from that of someone who appeared both overly skinny and malnourished to someone who could've competed on stage in a bikini competition if she wanted to. She trained hard with weights, whereas beforehand she had concentrated on long runs and spinning classes. She was soon squatting more than her bodyweight. By training with weights and eating well, we repaired her metabolism and then by eating on a sensible Calorie deficit we cut a bit of excess body fat and excess muscle and achieved the figure she had actually been craving all along but attempted to achieve in all the (classically) wrong ways. She has beaten the eating disorder and continues to make healthy choices while enjoying "naughty" food she would have abused in the past.

## 6.Mid thirties male - training and eating mistakes

This individual used the gym almost daily yet didn't have a physique that reflected that. He was knowledgeable and strong, but due to a complete lack of understanding of nutrition was not making the most of his training or the physique he was capable of. By utilising the ideas behind the 8 Simple Rules and 20 Foods to Eat and thus changing a more mainstream diet of processed foods and overeating, to restricted eating under maintenance Calories, over 3 months this individual displayed a cover model physique. He had to follow a hard training programme and devote a lot of time to this process, but the results were outstanding. With this change, the individual himself decided to take this further. He attempted multiple training programmes, tried various diets from IIFYM, to intermittent fasting, to cycling, all the time gaining muscle and at times leaning up considerably. He has since put himself on multiple courses and seminars in the nutrition and fitness industry and become a real voice of knowledge on nutrition and training in local gyms around his area. A simple 3month training plan and diet plan literally changed his life.

# About the Author

Sean Lerwill is a writer, cover model, actor, producer and health and fitness consultant from the UK.

Following his graduation from King's College London with a BSc (Hons) in Molecular Genetics, Sean served as an Officer in the Royal Marine Commandos earning his coveted Green Beret at the age of 22.

Sean chose to specialise as a Royal Marines Physical Training Instructor, earning his Crossed Clubs (the symbol of RM PTIs) and therefore the reputation of the Best Military Physical Trainers in the World.

During his time as a Royal Marines PTI Sean also qualified as a teacher, earning a Post Graduate Certificate of Education from the University of Plymouth in 2007.

In 2009 Sean was asked to write the Ministry of Defence backed: Haynes Guide to Royal Marines Fitness, published in January 2010 and soon became "the highlight of Haynes publishing year" that year. Following this, Sean left the British Forces to pursue a civilian career and start his own businesses.

Since becoming a civilian, Sean has written a further three books for Haynes and a book for Men's Fitness as well as produced numerous articles, programmes and supplements for national magazines and newspapers. Sean has also appeared on the covers of a number of fitness magazines in the UK and abroad.

In 2015 Sean published Pass the PRMC, a 26,000 word ebook full of hints and tips on how to pass the physical and mental tests expected of anyone wanting to join the Royal Marines Commandos.

Sean is a Maximuscle sponsored ambassador/spokesmodel providing expertise and advice for Maximuscle and other companies, including New Product Development and TeamBuilding/Leadership and Inspirational speaking.

# Web and Social Media

Website:         www.SeanLerwill.com

Facebook:             www.facebook.com/SeanLerwill

Twitter:         @SeanLerwill

Instagram:            @SeanLerwill

YouTube:              user/SeanLerwill

# Disclaimer and Copyright

Printed in Great
Britain
by Amazon